Building
a
Better
Vocabulary

Building a Better Vocabulary

Original title: *The Joy of Words*

HARRY SHAW

BARNES
&NOBLE
B O O K S
NEW YORK

Originally published as *The Joy of Words*

Copyright © 1984 by Harry Shaw

This edition published by Barnes & Noble, Inc.,
by arrangement with the Estate of Harry Shaw

1992 Barnes & Noble Books

ISBN 1-5661-9128-9

Printed and bound in the United States of America

01 02 MC 9 8 7 6 5

QF

Contents

1   Building and Using a Vocabulary   1

2   Make Friends with Your Dictionary   11

3   Extending the Range of Word
      Meanings   18

4   Losing a Vocabulary   22

5   Roots I   29

6   Roots II   37

7   Roots III   42

8   Roots IV   47

9   Combining Forms   53

10   Prefixes I   59

11   Prefixes II   65

12   Suffixes I   68

13   Suffixes II   73

14   Synonyms   76

15   Antonyms   81

16   Test Yourself   84

17   Fun with Words   102

Answers to *Quizzes*   111

Answers to *Test Yourself*   121

Answers to *Fun with Words*   124

**Building
a
Better
Vocabulary**

1

Building and Using a Vocabulary

"Don't you see what I mean?" "Why can't I explain this to you?" "It was the most . . . , er, well . . ." "If I could only say what I think . . ." "I know it but I can't say it."

Familiar phrases, aren't they? Never a day, hardly an hour, passes but we need to express some thought that seems difficult to put into words. The reason is clear: all our thinking is done in terms of concepts—words—and since we can't keep our minds still for long at any one time, we are constantly using words in our thinking and in our attempts to deliver our thoughts to others. Thinking and diction—which is the choice and use of words—go together. In a very real sense, thinking can be no more effective than the word supply behind it.

When you write a letter or join in a conversation, you *have* to have something to say and you *should* have some interest and

1

purpose in expressing that something, whatever it is. Therefore, you select those words at your command which will convey your meaning to others.

But most of us feel the weakness of our vocabulary at times. All of us have had the experience of not being able to find the right words to express our thoughts, of being misunderstood, of not being able to make ourselves clear. Since there is an almost complete interdependence between thought and language (Oliver Wendell Holmes once said, "A word is the skin of a living thought"), it follows that by using the most effective words possible we not only communicate our ideas more clearly to other people but also strengthen and clarify our own thinking.

Because it is difficult to think clearly and exactly, it is hard to achieve good diction. We make promises to recruit the vigor of our vocabulary. We are aware that our lack of mastery of words prevents our full possession of hundreds of impressions, thoughts, and feelings which come to us from observation and thinking. But although we wish to increase and strengthen our vocabularies, few of us are willing to make a real effort to do so. Do not be misled; there are no quick methods of acquiring and mastering a good vocabulary. Occasionally looking up a word in the dictionary will help very little. Sitting down in a burst of enthusiasm to memorize scores of words from it is also valueless. The most direct attack upon the problem is to learn to utilize words that we already have in our potential vocabularies.

Each of us has three vocabularies. First, there is our *active,* or *speaking,* vocabulary. This is our word stock, the words we use daily in speaking. Second, there is our *writing* vocabulary. This is also active in that we use its word supply in writing. It contains many words we do not use in speech. In addition to these two active, or productive, vocabularies each of us has a *potential* or *recognition* vocabulary, the largest of the three. By means of this potential vocabulary, we can understand speakers and books, magazines, and newspapers. Still, in our reading and listening we encounter many words that we recognize and partly understand, possibly from context, but which we would not be able to use in our own speaking and writing. Until we use such words, however—start them working for *us*—they are not really ours.

Effort is needed to move words from our potential to our active vocabulary. But it is the logical way to begin vocabulary improvement, for the good reason that words in a recognition vocabulary, having made some impression on our consciousness, are already partly ours. Their values, although still vague to us, can be made exact and accurate. Furthermore, quite likely they are words that we will want in our vocabularies. Probably we have come across them time and again; they are not unusual and high-sounding words. They are words that have *use* value. Mastering them will help us to avoid the pitfall of "swallowing the dictionary," a task that fails because it has no direct connection with our needs.

We have both to learn, and to learn how to use, words before they can become part of our active vocabularies. A teacher recently told one of his students that he felt the student was using words that he did not really understand. The student protested that he did know the meanings of the words, that many of them were words he had noted in his regular reading of a well-known weekly magazine. The instructor commended the student for his enterprise, and then requested that he read the current issue of the magazine over the weekend and bring his copy to class on the following Monday. The teacher also got the issue and read it carefully. He marked 102 words, some of which he had to look up in a dictionary himself, but most of which he felt certain the student did not know. On Monday, the instructor underlined the 102 words in the student's copy and requested the student to give a working definition of each and to use it in a sentence. Half an hour later, the student announced that he could define and use only about half of them. He was told to

3

define as many as he could. After cutting down the number several times, he finally managed to define roughly and use correctly only eight of the words! He was an intelligent student; the magazine was widely circulated and was written for popular consumption; the great majority of the words were not unusual; he had simply assumed that he knew words that he did not know. They had some recognition value for him, but no *use* value. After being cautioned not to learn all the 102 words (a few were esoteric), he set out to master the others, thus moving them from his potential to his active vocabulary.

Actually, acquiring an active vocabulary of considerable range is not so formidable a task as it may seem when you are looking at a huge, unabridged dictionary. A reliable scholar has revealed that even Shakespeare, that master of diction, used fewer than 17,000 words in all his plays. And yet the average American knows about 10,000 words—the words most common in newspapers, general magazines, and daily speaking.

Certain quality magazines such as *The Atlantic Monthly* and *Harper's* assume that their readers command the vocabulary of the average college graduate: 20,000 to 25,000 words. However, a number of careful studies have revealed that certain basic words are used most frequently in writing and speaking. One such study, Thorndike and Lorge's *The Teacher's Word Book of 30,000 Words,* contains from 10,000 to 15,000 words that are known to nearly every adult and are commonly used. It is reasonable to assume, therefore, that you have a vocabulary of at least this size. With this number as a starter, you can begin to build.

Building and using a vocabulary is indeed worthwhile, but there's no need to get an anxiety fit about doing this. Actually, you know and can use accurately most of the words you hear and read. How can this be?

Of course we do hear and come across in reading words that are new and unknown to us. But isn't it comforting to know that only twelve simple words account for one-fourth of everything spoken and written in English? What are the words most often used? Simple indeed: *a, and, he, I, in, it, is, of, that, the, to, was.* These twelve words and thirty-eight more make up half the running total in *all* English speech and writing. If you increase the number to the one thousand most common words in English, you will account for 80 percent of the words *everyone* uses in speaking and writing and encounters in reading.

Are you inclined to doubt these statements? They have been verified and substantiated by the word count of Professors Thorndike and Lorge mentioned earlier. Over the years, other experts have unhesitatingly accepted the findings of these scholars. And just so you will be relieved about learning some of the words you *don't* know, here are the one thousand most commonly used words in English speech and writing, listed in two degrees of popularity. You probably know every one of them.

Words preceding the semicolon appear in the first 500 words most used. Words following the semicolon appear in the second 500 words most used.

a, about, above, across, act, add, after, again, against, age, ago, air, all, almost, alone, along, already, also, always, am, America, American, among, an, and, another, answer, any, anything, appear, are, arm, army, around, as, ask, at, away; able, accept, according, account, action, admit, advance, affair, afternoon, afraid, agree, allow, although, amount, animal, arrive, art, Arthur, article, attempt

back, bank, be, became, because, become, been, before, began, begin, being, believe, best, better, between, big, bill, body, book, both, boy, bring, brought, built, business, but, by; baby, bad, bag, ball, battle, bay, bear, beat, beautiful, beauty, bed, behind, belong, below, beside, beyond, bird, bit, black, blood, blow, blue, board, boat, born, box, branch, break, bridge, bright, British, broken, brother, brown, build, building, burn, busy, buy

call, came, can, car, care, carry, case, cause, chance, change, child, children, city, close, color, come, coming, company, condition, consider, continue, cost, could, country, course, court, cover, cry, cut; cannot, can't, captain, catch, caught, cent, center, century, certain, certainly, chain, chair, character, charge, Chicago, chief, church, circle, class, clean, clear, clothes, cloud, club, coal, coat, cold, college, command, common, complete, contain, control, cook, cool, corner, count, cross, crowd, cup

day, dear, demand, did, die, different, do, doctor, does, dollar, done, don't, door, down, dress, drop, during; dance, dare, dark, date, daughter, dead, deal, death, decide, declare, deep, degree, desire, destroy, difference, dinner, direct, direction, discover, distance, dog, double, doubt, draw, dream, drink, drive, dry, due, duty

each, early, either, end, enough, even, evening, ever, every, everything, eye; ear, earth, east, easy, eat, edge, effort, egg, eight, else, enemy, England, English, enjoy, enter, escape, especially, Europe, except, expect, experience, explain, express

face, fact, fall, family, far, father, fear, feel, feet, felt, few, fight, figure, fill, find, fine, fire, first, five, follow, food, for, force, found, four, friend, from, front, full; fail, fair, famous, farm, farmer, fast, favor, fell, fellow, field, finally, finger, finish, fish, fit, floor, flower, fly, fool, foot, foreign, forest, forget, form, forth, forward, France, free, French, fresh, fruit, further, future garden, gave, get, girl, give, given, go, God, gone, good, got, government, great, green; gain, game, gate, gather, general, gentleman, George, German, Germany, glad, glass, going, gold, golden, grant, grass, gray, grew, ground, group, grow, guard, guess, guide

had, half, hand, happen, happy, hard, has, have, he, head, hear, heard, heart, held, help, her, here, herself, high, him, himself, his, hold, home, hope, horse, hour, house, how, however, human, hundred, husband; hair, hall, hang, hat, health, heat, heaven, heavy, height, Henry, hill, history, hole, honor, hot, hurry, hurt

I, idea, if, I'll, important, in, increase, interest, into, is, it, its, itself; ice, ill, inch, include, indeed, Indian, industry, instead, iron, island, issue

John, just; job, join, joy, judge

keep, kept, kind, king, knew, know; kill, kiss, kitchen, knee, knight, known

labor, lady, land, large, last, late, laugh, law, learn, least, leave, left, less, let, letter, lie, life, light, like, line, little, live, long, look, lost, love, low; laid, lake, lay, lead, led, leg, length, lift, lip, listen, London, lord, lose, loss, lot, lower

made, make, man, many, mark, marry, matter, may, me, mean, men, might, mile, mind, miss, moment, money, month, more, morning, most, mother, move, Mr., Mrs., much, must, my, myself; manner, march, market, Mary, master, material, measure, meat, meet, meeting, member, met, method, middle, milk, million, mine, minute, modern, mount, mountain, mouth, movement, music name, national, near, need, never, new, New York, next, night, no, nor, not, note, nothing, now, number; nation, natural, nature, nearly, necessary, neck, neighbor, neither, news, nice, nine, none, north, nose, notice

of, off, office, often, old, on, once, one, only, open, or, order, other, our, out, over, own; O, object, obtain, ocean, offer, officer, oh, oil, opinion, ought, outside

paper, part, party, pass, pay, people, perhaps, person, picture, place, plan, plant, play, point, poor, possible, power, present, president, price, produce, public, put; page, paid, pain, paint, pair, past, peace, period, pick, piece, plain, pleasant, please, pleasure, position, post, pound, practice, prepare, press, pretty, prince, probably, problem, promise, prove, provide, pull, purpose

question, quite; quarter, queen, quickly

rather, reach, read, real, reason, receive, red, remain, remember, rest, result, return, right, river, road, room, round, run; race, rain, raise, ran, ready, realize, really, record, refuse, regard, reply, report, require, rich, ride, ring, rise, rock, roll, rose, rule, rush

said, same, sat, saw, say, school, sea, second, see, seem, seen, serve, set, several, shall, she, ship, short, should, show, side, since, sir, small, smile, so, some, something, son, soon, sort, sound, speak, stand, start, state, step, still, stood, stop, story, street, strong, such, sun, supply, suppose, sure, system; safe, sail, salt, save, scene, season, seat, seek, sell, send, sense, sent, service, settle, seven, shade, shape, share, shoe, shop, shore, shot, shoulder, shout, sick, sight, sign, silver, simple, sing, single, sister, sit, six, size, skin, sky, sleep, smoke, snow, soft, soil, sold, soldier, sometimes, song, soul, south, space, special, spend, spirit, spoke, spot, spread, spring, square, St., star, station, stay, stick, stock, stone, store, storm, straight, strange, stream, strength, study, subject, success, sudden, suddenly, suffer, sugar, suit, summer, surprise, sweet

table, take, taken, talk, tell, ten, than, that, the, their, them, themselves, then, there, these, they, thing, think, this, those, though, thought, thousand, three, through, thus, time, to, today, together, told, too, took, toward, town, tree, tried, true, try, turn, twenty, two; tall, taste, teach, tear, thank, thee, therefore, thin, third, thirty, thou, tie, till, tire (d), tomorrow, top, touch, trade, train, travel, trip, trouble, trust, truth, twelve

under, until, up, upon, us, use; uncle, understand, usually

very, voice; valley, value, various, view, village, visit

wait, walk, wall, want, war, was, Washington, watch, water, way, we, week, well, went, were, what, when, where, whether, which, while, white, who, whole, whom, whose, why, wife, will, wind, window, wish, with, within, without, woman, women, wonder, word, work, world, would, write, wrong; warm, wave, wear, weather, weight, west, wide, wild, wing (ed), winter, wise, wonderful, won't, wood, worth

year, yes, yet, you, young, your; yard, yellow, yourself

That only one thousand words make up 80 percent of the words used in speaking and writing does not mean that in any particular conversation, lecture, talk, or piece of writing these words would appear in precisely that percentage. Nor does this basic fact have any bearing upon two other considerations: (1)

some of the remaining 20 percent do involve problems and (2) the actual words comprising this remaining 20 percent may differ widely with individual speakers and writers.

Doesn't it help to know that 80 percent of your job is completed before you start and that you can have fun, pleasure, and even excitement as you tackle the remaining part of the task?

The purpose of this book is simple: to help you improve your knowledge of the English language by mastering whatever part of the 20 percent of unknown words you need in your speaking and writing. If you are a poor speaker, this book will help you become a better one. If you already speak well, it will help you to talk even more effectively.

Several ways of building a vocabulary have been tried and are listed below. For some persons, one or more of them have proved useful.

1. Learning lists of unfamiliar words, usually by concentrated dictionary study
2. Listing and studying words heard on the radio and television and come across in reading
3. Studying new subjects on your own or in a class
4. Studying the meanings of words beyond their primary and commonly accepted meanings
5. Studying word-building devices such as *combining forms, prefixes,* and *suffixes*
6. Mastering lists of *synonyms* and *antonyms*
7. Studying Latin, Greek, and other word elements, such as *roots*

The first of these seven methods is not recommended because it wastes time and is self-defeating. The other six approaches get their full share of attention in the chapters that follow.

2

Make Friends with Your Dictionary

The natural and commonsense way to gain a good vocabulary is to absorb words steadily from wide reading. But if time has passed you by and you need a more direct and quicker way to acquire word power, the following steps will help. They are indeed the methods stressed in this book.

1. The study of word *roots*
2. The study of *combining forms*
3. The study of *prefixes*
4. The study of *suffixes*
5. The study of *synonyms*
6. The study of *antonyms*

Each of these six approaches involves careful and consistent use of a good dictionary. Rule 1 in vocabulary improvement is MAKE FRIENDS WITH YOUR DICTIONARY. Do not,

11

however, make the mistake of trying to "swallow the dictionary." This marvelous tool of learning should be used in definite, specific ways that have nothing to do with trying to master scores of words without any specific plan or pattern.

Suitable dictionaries are what economists refer to as "durable goods." When you purchase a good dictionary, you should expect to keep and use it for many years. It is unwise to buy a "cheap" dictionary when the price of an excellent one is not great considering that the cost can be amortized over a long period. A pocket dictionary is almost worthless, except as a flimsy guide to spelling and pronunciation. Equip yourself with a sufficiently large dictionary (approximately 100,000 entries), published by a reliable firm.

If you have never done so before, examine your dictionary carefully and critically. Read its table of contents; check the information given on the inside of front and back covers; skim the introductory pages as well as any supplementary materials at the back. Then read thoughtfully any editorial sections it contains: "General Introduction," "Guide to the Use of this Dictionary," "Guide to Pronunciation," or "Explanatory Notes." You may be astonished to discover resources of which you were previously unaware.

You should actually *study* each word you look up. Take your time; it requires only a moment to learn the spelling, pronunciation, or one meaning of a word. But hasty examination will prevent your mastering the word and making it a part of your active vocabulary, and it will thwart any hope of your greeting the word as a familiar friend when next you meet it in an unfamiliar context. Time spent in learning words thoroughly will save time, errors, and annoyance later.

For any word listed in an adequate dictionary, each of the first five of the following items is given. For many words, some of the next five kinds of information is provided:

1.	Spelling	6.	Level(s) of meaning
2.	Syllabication	7.	Derivation (origin)
3.	Pronunciation	8.	Synonyms
4.	Part(s) of speech	9.	Antonyms
5.	Meaning(s)	10.	Other information

If while reading you dislike breaking the chain of thought by looking up words in a dictionary (although the very necessity for using a dictionary has already broken that chain), jot down unfamiliar words and look them up as soon as possible. Keeping a notebook nearby is a good idea. Set down the unfamiliar words you come across as you read and look them up later. Be sure, after you have thoroughly studied a new word, to use it in speaking and writing until it is yours. Adding words to one's stock can be fascinating, but there must be a systematic and constant exercise of your *will* to study and use what you have acquired.

Each of the chapters that follows requires you to consult your dictionary. Doing so will be both rewarding and interesting. The book now in your hands is largely a carefully planned series of dictionary studies, a plot to get you to think of your dictionary as a constant companion, a close friend, an ever-present ally as you increase your word power. The book you are now reading will be almost useless to you unless you resolve to use your dictionary on an almost constant basis.

Try to master the new words you meet not only because doing so will enhance your reading, writing, and speaking but because a good vocabulary will be increasingly important in your life. Johnson O'Connor, a scientific investigator, has stated:

An extensive knowledge of the exact meanings of English words accompanies outstanding success in this country more often than any other single characteristic which the Human Engineering Laboratory has been able to isolate and measure.

QUIZ 1

Read carefully every word on *one* page of your dictionary. Here's a guarantee: you will be surprised at what you discover about the origin and meaning of at least three entries.

QUIZ 2

Supply the missing word from each of the lists given. Choose the word that most nearly fits the meaning of the sentence. (More than one choice may be possible.)

1. We have decided to ignore his comment, and nothing he can say will _____ us to reply.
   (a) aggravate (b) irritate (c) provoke (d) exasperate

2. It's harder to be patient under long-continuing _____ than to face a momentary danger boldly.
   (a) calamity (b) misfortune (c) disaster (d) mischance

3. Carrying the surveying equipment proved exhausting, and before we had gone far I began to wish I had chosen a less _____ load.
   (a) heavy (b) weighty (c) ponderous (d) cumbersome

4. She decided to spend the morning in an aimless _____ through surrounding fields and woods.
   (a) ramble (b) excursion (c) tour (d) trip

5. For a long time his conscience continued to ——————— him for having betrayed his better nature.
   (a) censure   (b) condemn   (c) reprove   (d) reproach

QUIZ 3

Supply the missing word from the list given. Choose the word that most exactly fits the meaning of the sentence. (More than one choice can be defended.)

1. Inside the door we were met by a really mouth-watering (a: smell; b: scent; c: odor; d: perfume; e: aroma).

2. I find that tight little self-satisfied (a: smile; b: grin; c: simper; d: smirk; e: grimace) of his after a supposed witticism extremely annoying.

3. I know and have studied all the facts in the case, and nothing you can say will shake my (a: opinion; b: belief; c: conviction; d: view; e: sentiment) that he is innocent.

4. The work that I had found so interesting at first became by repetition a mindless and disagreeable (a: task; b: chore; c: stint; d: assignment; e: job).

5. The course of the debate revealed ever more widely (a: different; b: diverse; c: divergent; d: distinct; e: dissimilar) views on the two sides of the aisle, and it was clear that no agreement would be possible.

QUIZ 4

Supply the missing word from the list given. Choose the word that most exactly fits the meaning of the sentence. (More than one choice is possible.)

1. Terry, Michael, and I—scrubbed, dressed up, and sworn to good behavior until the ceremony was over—sat prim and (a: serious; b: earnest; c: grave; d: sedate; e: solemn) in the front row.

2. Claims that he had accepted support from radicals of the extreme right were indignantly (a: declined; b: refused; c: rejected; d: repudiated; e: spurned) by the candidate as false and malicious.

3. The lieutenant of detectives admitted that his men were (a: frustrated; b: baffled; c: balked; d: foiled; e: thwarted) by the absence of clues and the lack of any credible motive for the crime.

4. He scattered their favorite food in the clearing in order to (a: lure; b: inveigle; c: entice; d: beguile; e: tempt) the birds to approach within camera range.

5. The distinction between one insect species and another often depends on (a: little; b: small; c: tiny; d: minute; e: diminutive) differences in structure or coloration.

QUIZ 5

What is the derivation (origin) of the following words?

1. telescope   3. manufacture   5. nicotine
2. panic   4. professor   6. April

QUIZ 6

What is the past tense and past participle of each of these verbs? Do you have a dictionary handy?

1.	attack	6.	leap	11.	make	16.	pay
2.	dive	7.	swear	12.	send	17.	fight
3.	wring	8.	awake	13.	win	18.	bring
4.	draw	9.	smell	14.	spell	19.	come
5.	bite	10.	set	15.	take	20.	grow

QUIZ 7

Use your knowledge and your dictionary to form plurals of

1.	analysis	5.	leaf	9.	hypothesis	13.	crisis
2.	antenna	6.	stratus	10.	criterion	14.	spoonful
3.	mongoose	7.	half	11.	summons	15.	stimulus
4.	moose	8.	phenom-enon	12.	alumnus		

baffle. to frustrate or check (a person) by confusing or perplexing

balk - to stop short and refuse to go on.

foil. to prevent from being successful

diminutive - extremly small in size

17

3

Extending the Range of Word Meanings

Most common words have meanings that are generally recognized, understood, and accepted. And yet we tend to overlook areas of meaning that most words have beyond their primary import. When looking up a word in a dictionary all too often we notice one meaning and are content with that, overlooking additional applications and meanings that would greatly extend our vocabulary.

Some scholars feel that widening and sharpening our knowledge of the meanings of ordinary words is an unexcelled way to build a vocabulary. Of course it's possible to increase one's word hoard by adding additional units of words. And yet to push first the addition of more vocabulary units in order to increase the number of words may sometimes interfere with our mastery of language.

The five hundred words most frequently used in the English language (see Chapter 1) have a total of 14,070 separate meanings as listed in the *Oxford English Dictionary*. If this statement sounds unbelievable, just consider the simple, every-day word *count*. As a verb, noun, and adjective *count* has twenty-eight listed meanings in the desk dictionary nearest the writer's hand. An illustration: "The children did not count" can mean that the children were "not considered" or that they did not "utter the words for numbers in a series."

Again, "to count on" is "to rely" or "depend" on. To "count out" is "to exclude" or "to disqualify" or "to declare a loser." As a noun, "count" can mean "the act of counting," "enumeration," "an accounting," "a charge in a declaration of legal indictment," "a number representing the size and quality of yarn," and have still other meanings and applications in physics, bowling, and boxing. As an adjective, "count" refers to the number of items determined by actual count: "The container is labeled '100 count'."

It's hard to believe that such an everyday word can have so many meanings. But what is true of *count* is true of thousands of other common words. One important way to sharpen our observation of the great range of meanings covered by a single vocabulary item is to collect instances of the same word. The four-letter word *turn* provides a good example:

"She made a sudden *turn,* as if to speak."
"The rest of the party had vanished around a *turn* in the road."
"All his fortune was lost by a *turn* of the dice."
"They said they would take a *turn* around the garden before going in."

"We hesitated whether to go on or *turn* back."
"The manufacturers have had their *turn;* now we must
consider the farmers."
"It was only a dream but it gave me a terrible *turn.*"

The purpose of such a study as this is to suggest that in
consulting a dictionary one should consider the complete entry
for a word and not be content with only one or two meanings
and also to cause one to understand and accept important considerations about the range and richness of the English language. Only such careful study of dictionary entries can help us
overcome the misunderstandings and confusions that lie in
everyday words.

Studying the areas of meaning for words already known in
their primary sense is as productive as adding completely new
units to vocabulary stock. The simple word *set* is surely in
everyone's everyday vocabulary. And yet it is worth noting that
this little three-letter word has 115 distinct meanings and applications as listed in *The Random House Dictionary of the English
Language.* As a noun, verb, adjective, and interjection, *set* has
separate applications in such areas as surgery, music, carpentry,
horticulture, psychology, painting, bridge, hair styling, stamp
collecting, machinery, sailing, and the game of tennis.

Or consider the simple word *cold.* As an adjective, noun,
and adverb it is given twenty-eight separate listings in a widely
used dictionary. Many of these meanings are related to each other,
but they have individual applications and connotations:

My hands are *cold.*
The deed was done in *cold* blood.
I learned that lesson *cold.*
The atmosphere in the room was *cold.*
The boxer was out *cold.*
I feel as if I'm catching a *cold.*

That winter we suffered from the extreme *cold*.
Did you just leave the job *cold?*
The dogs soon lost the *cold* scent.
I admire the *cold* precision of your speech.

Notice the different meanings and applications of *cold* in these often-used expressions:

cold shoulder, cold cuts, cold sore, cold storage, cold wave, cold logic, cold color, cold sober, cold chisel, cold cream, cold frame, cold war, cold deck, cold steel, cold sweat, cold turkey, cold patch, cold feet, cold comfort, cold light

Take your time when you look up a word. Read the complete dictionary entry. Get hold of some of the multiple meanings that most words have. There is no easier or more effective way to add to your vocabulary.

QUIZ 8

In a widely used dictionary, the entry *run* has 172 listed meanings. Go through your dictionary to find other words with many meanings and uses. Select *one* of the words you find and study it carefully. No matter what the word is, if you study it carefully you will add considerably to your vocabulary and knowledge of word study.

4
Losing a
Vocabulary

Although using an enlarged and improved vocabulary is highly important, "losing" a vocabulary also deserves attention. The problem of diction (the choice and use of words) is somewhat similar to that of managing a store. The storekeeper has to keep replenishing his stock, but he also has to get rid of certain items that have proved unsatisfactory. He has to know what stock will be salable to what customers at what seasons of the year. He tries to keep in stock all the items for which there will be a demand, but frequently he has to place a rush order with a wholesaler for something not on his shelves.

So it is with our diction. We stock our word supplies as well as we can; we constantly replenish our stock; we cease using certain words as we find others that are more effective; we realize that certain words will serve on one occasion and not on another; and we frequently find that; no matter how large our vocabularies, we have to put in "rush orders" to dictionaries.

The problem of diction is, first, acquiring a good stock of

words; second, eliminating from our use certain words and expressions that do not come up to acceptable standards; third, choosing from our own stock or from dictionaries and similar books those words that will most correctly, clearly, and forcefully express our meaning.

No standards of diction can be absolute, but it is safe to say that good English is English used by reputable speakers and writers. Such usage is never fixed, but changes constantly, as the product of custom or appropriateness of words in relation to context. For speakers' and writers' vocabularies are the *number* of words they can command; diction is the *kind* of words used. Words once considered not acceptable are now sanctioned, and vice versa. Diction ranges from philosophical abstractness to racy slang, from lofty Shakespearean utterances to the dialect of *Huckleberry Finn*. No single kind, in itself, is "good" or "bad," for a word perfect in one context may be inappropriate in another. But there are three general principles that apply to correct usage, which have remained constant and serve as guides: Words should be in *present* use, in *national* use, and in *reputable* use. It is possible that you use words that violate one or more of these principles. If so, weed out such words and expressions; at least, be on guard when you desire to use them.

1. Slang

Slang is defined as language that consists of widely current terms having forced or fantastic meaning, or displaying eccentricity. It is markedly colloquial language below the range of standard or cultivated speech.

The characteristics of slang include flippant or eccentric humor; forced, fantastic, or grotesque meanings; novelty; attempts to be vivid, fresh, pungent, colorful. Such expressions may appeal to the popular fancy or to some segment of it (college slang, Army slang, Navy slang, baseball slang), but in general they are substandard. Even so, slang may for a time be used over a wide area, and a considerable number of words and phrases bear the "slang" label in our dictionaries. If such expressions persist, they may eventually receive the respectable label "colloquial."

Slang is popular, but sound reasons exist for avoiding it, or at least its overuse. First, much slang lasts for a brief time only and then passes out of use. (Think for a moment: what expressions have you stopped using because others have taken their place?) Second, using slang expressions often prevents us from searching for the exact words needed to express meaning. That is, many slang terms are only "rubber stamps." Third, slang short-circuits the primary purpose of speaking—conveying a clear and exact meaning.

Reasons exist for the careful and sparing use of slang. It *does* avoid wordiness. It *does* avoid artificiality. In informal speaking among friends, occasional use of such words as "uppers" (amphetamines), "legit," "snafu," "off the wall," "freak out," "ripped off," and "pad" is permissible. But note the caution: *occasional*. And don't let a fondness for slang and its ease of use stop you from searching for better ways to express what you have in mind.

2. Triteness

Trite or hackneyed expressions, or clichés, are words that have lost their force through overuse. The origins of the words *triteness*, *hackneyed*, and *cliché* are illuminating: the first comes from the Latin word *tritus*, the past participle of *terere*, which means "to rub," "to wear out"; *hackneyed* is derived from the idea of a horse, or carriage, let out for hire, devoted to common use, and thus worn out in service; *cliché* comes from the French word *clicher*, meaning "to stereotype, to cast from a mold, to use over and over."

Thus trite words and phrases are but rubber stamps or stereotyped plates of thought and expression. They may be tags from common speech, or overworked quotations, or outworn phrases from newspapers. They save the writer the trouble of thinking and expressing exactly what he means, but their use results in writing that is stale and ineffective. Such words and phrases inevitably seem humorous; they are, indeed, regularly used for humor or irony by fiction writers and columnists. Used seriously, they are signs that the speaker, or writer, is naïve.

Here are a dozen trite expressions that illustrate how weary and dull our talk can be:

> a bolt from the blue, checkered career, depths of despair,
> green as grass, heartfelt thanks, last straw, fair sex,
> clinging vine, sadder but wiser, needs no introduction,
> time marches on, safe to say

Such expressions make sense and are in no sense incorrect. What's wrong with them is that they are not crisp and fresh. The ease and regularity with which we use them prevents us from searching for more exact and emphatic expressions.

Our familiarity with trite words and expressions is likely to cause them to occur to us more readily than others, which are more effective. We should look with suspicion upon each word or phrase that leaps to mind until we can assure ourselves that the expression is exact, fresh, and unhackneyed. It is also well to remember that words and phrases which do not seem trite to us may be clichés to anyone more familiar with overworked expressions.

3. Exaggeration

Unless used for deliberate effect, *exaggeration* is misleading because it is inexact and even ludicrous: "As a youngster I used

laughable or hilarious because of obvious absurdity or incongruity 25 to die laughing at my father's jokes.'' It will greatly improve your choice and use of words if you will avoid all but occasional use of words such as *terrible, ghastly, horrible, thrilling, marvelous, gorgeous, amazing, awful, splendid,* and *phenomenal.* These and similar words have their legitimate uses but have been used inexactly so often that they are rarely effective.

4. Idiom

Idiom means the forms or variety of expression of a language, the characteristic way in which it is put together. In speaking of French idiom, for example, we refer to such a distinct usage as putting the adjective after its noun or the fact that an adjective in French has forms for singular and plural and for masculine and feminine gender. *An* idiom, as distinct from *idiom,* is a structural form peculiar to a language. Normally, an idiom is an accepted word or phrase that violates grammar, or logic, or both.

Idiomatic usage should conform to the word links generally acceptable. A good dictionary will contain a statement of idiomatic usage following entries needing such explanations. You should ''lose'' from your vocabulary such unidiomatic expressions as those in this left-hand column:

Unidiomatic	*Idiomatic*
accord to	accord with
according with	according to
accuse with	accuse of
acquitted from	acquitted of
adverse against	adverse to
aim at proving	aim to prove
frightened of	frightened by, at
graduated (high school)	graduated from (high school)
have got to	must

26

identical to	identical with
in accordance to	in accordance with
jealous for	jealous of
kind of a	kind of
listen at	listen to
monopoly for, on	monopoly of
oblivious to	oblivious of
on line	in line
out loud	aloud
prefer (one) over (another)	prefer to
prior than	prior to
providing	provided
sensitive about (a stimulus)	sensitive to
superior than	superior to
tend to	attend to
to home	at home
treat on (a subject)	treat of
try and	try to

5. Tired words

We use an astonishingly small number of words and we use them over and over again. Through habit, we usually continue to say about the same thing in about the same words. It's human nature (because it's easy) to use the first words that come to mind. One excellent way to improve the quality of one's vocabulary is to avoid using weary, overworked words and to search for expressions that are more exact, more colorful, or more emphatic.

To determine the exact word needed, you must become aware of shades of meaning, of distinctions that clarify the idea for which you wish to use the word as symbol. When you want to describe a surface that, from every point of view, lies on a line corresponding to or parallel with the horizon, will you use *flat, plane, level, even, flush,* or *smooth?* Always choose the word that shows most exactly the meaning you intend.

The following words and expressions are not incorrect and are occasionally needed. But it's advisable to stop overusing them:

funny	and everything	factor
crazy	slick	character
fine	and such	fix
nice	scared	party
grand	bad	get
good	thing	lazy
you know	old	awfully
instance	very	case
nature	afraid	proposition
condition	guess	o.k.

"Losing a vocabulary" may seem a negative approach, but getting rid of deadwood will make room for the newly acquired words and expressions that will enrich your vocabulary.

QUIZ 9

Some words are limited to a particular region, subject, time, or level of usage. In a dictionary you may find labels indicating such limitations as "Brit" (for Great Britain), "obs" (for obsolete), and "chem" (for chemistry). What restrictive label, if any, is attached to each of the following entries in your dictionary?

1. baloney
2. cocky - *over self confident*
3. disremember - *to fail to remember*
4. jiffy - *a short space of time, a mo*
5. pesky - *troublesome, annoying*
6. auld - *old*

5

Roots I

One of the easiest, most useful, and quickest ways to build a vocabulary is to learn how words are put together. Once you recognize the elements—the building blocks—of which words are made, hundreds, even thousands, of unfamiliar words will begin to have meaning for you.

The first and probably most important building block for words is *roots*. A root is the part of a word that indicates its primary, essential meaning. This meaning never changes, no matter what other letters and word parts are added. (Such additions as *prefixes* and *suffixes*, two other building blocks, are treated later in this book.)

Consider the root *vit-*, also spelled *viv-*, meaning "to live" or "life." From this building block come such words as these:

1. **vital**—*(vit-* means "life"; the suffix *-al* means "pertaining to." Thus *vital* means necessary to life, full of life, or pertaining to life.

2. **vitamin**—*(vit-* plus the suffix *-amin)*. A *vitamin* is a substance in food either useful or necessary for normal life in human beings and animals.

3. **vivacious**—a word meaning lively, active, full of life.
4. **vivid**—a word meaning lifelike, lively.
5. **revive**—a word formed from *viv-* and the prefix *re-*, meaning to bring back to life, to live again.

Other words formed from *vit-* are: *vivacity, vivisection, vivify, survival, vitality, revival, vitalize,* and *viviparous.* Note how knowing the meaning of this one root, *vit-*, makes clear the meaning of useful words perhaps unknown before.

Scores of word roots exist in English and are listed and defined in all superior dictionaries. When you come across a word that you suspect may be built from a root, try to find the part of the word you think is a root and consult your dictionary. Developing the habit of doing this will tremendously increase your vocabulary in easy, fun-producing steps.

Of the hundred or so most common roots in English, this book selects twenty for discussion in this and the next three chapters. Study these four chapters carefully. Mastering them will help you to add hundreds of words to your active vocabulary. But don't stop with your study of these twenty roots. Enormous riches lie in other word roots, the meaning and use of which are easily discovered in your dictionary.

1. anim-

This root comes from Latin, in which the word *animus* meant "that which blows (wind) or is breathed (air)." In English, *anim-* means "soul," "life," "spirit." Note its appearance in these words:

1. **animate** means "to give life to," "to make alive." Her appearance *animated* the party. He was *animated* by a de-

sire to win. As an adjective *animate* means "alive" or "lively." Her laughter was an *animate* expression of her pleasure. Words related to *animate* are *animated, animation,* and *inanimate* (meaning "lifeless").

2. **animosity** means "a feeling of ill will or enmity." The word formerly meant "having a high or lively spirit" but is now used to mean "vigorous dislike." The old settler felt *animosity* toward the newcomers.

3. **animal** means "any living thing or being." It includes, in addition to humans, any living object: a fish, a bird, or an insect. All men, women, and children are *animals*. What's your favorite *animal* in the zoo? Related words are *animality* (animal nature) and *animalistic* (like an animal). *Animalism* is defined as "preoccupation with physical or sensual appetites."

4. **unanimous** means "of a mind," "agreed," "in complete accord." The word is built from the Latin prefix *un-* (meaning "one"), the root *anim-* ("spirit," "mind," "heart"), and the suffix *-ous* ("being," "having"). The vote for the motion was *unanimous*. A related word is *unanimity*.

5. **equanimity** means "composure," "stability," "calmness." It comes from *equ-* ("even," "equal") and *anim-*: The speaker listened with *equanimity* to catcalls and shouts from the audience.

2. annu-

The root *annu-* (also spelled "enni-") means "year."

1. **annual** means "yearly," "occurring or returning once a year." It is from the root *annu-* plus the Latin suffix *-al*. In botany, *annual* means "lasting only one year." The word

also means "a pamphlet, periodical, or book published once a year." This company allows an *annual* vacation of three weeks. Corn is an *annual* crop.

2. **annuity** means "a specified income payable at stated intervals," the intervals usually being one year. Her *annuity* will last for a lifetime.

3. **biennial** means "happening, lasting, or enduring for two years." It is made up of the prefix *bi-* ("two") and *enni:* This is a *biennial* convention, taking place in even-numbered years.

4. **annals** means "a yearly record of events," although its meaning has been extended to cover greater periods of time and frequently the word is applied to historical and other records: the *annals* of war, the *annals* of American history.

5. **centennial** comes from the Latin root *cent-* (meaning "one hundred") and *enni-*. The word means "lasting one hundred years," "a hundredth celebration or anniversary," "happening once every hundred years." The *centennial* of the founding of this town was celebrated a year ago.

3. bene-

This Latin root means "well," "good," "helpful."
It is the basic element of many everyday words.

1. **benefit** comes from *bene-* plus "fit," which derives from a Latin word meaning "to make," "to do." A *benefit* is an act of kindness, a good deed, "anything that promotes well-being." The auction was held for the *benefit* of our church. We hope to *benefit* from your advice.

2. **beneficial** derives from the same elements as "benefit," plus the suffix *-ial. Beneficial* means "helpful," "advan-

tageous," "promoting a favorable result." Exercise is considered *beneficial* to one's health.

3. **benediction** is derived from *bene-*, the Latin root *dict-* (meaning "to say," "to speak"), and the suffix *-ion*. A *benediction* is "a blessing," "the act of blessing." The minister closed the exercises with a *benediction*.

4. **benevolent** is made up of *bene-* and Latin *volent-*, meaning "willing." *Benevolent* is used to mean "kindly," "disposed to do good," "charitable." Mother felt *benevolent* toward the homeless children. Some lodges and fraternities are *benevolent* aid societies.

5. **benefactor** comes from *bene-* and a Latin word meaning "someone who does." A *benefactor* is someone who does good deeds, is a supporter of good causes. The art museum needs more *benefactors*. My *benefactor* gave me money for some new clothes.

Other words using the root *bene-* are beneficiary, benefaction, benefactress, benefice, beneficent, benevolence, and the related term *benign*.

4. cred-

This root means "to trust," "to believe."

1. **credentials** comes from *cred-* and the suffixes *-ent* and *-al*. The word means anything that provides the basis for confidence, belief, and credit. It also means "evidence of authority, rights, and status." Only those with proper *credentials* will be admitted. Her *credentials* as a judge are superior.

2. **credit** comes from *cred-* and has several meanings: trustworthiness, credibility; acknowledgment of having done something creditable; time allowed for payment; confi-

dence in a person's ability to perform or pay; to accept as true. He deserves *credit* for his effort. His *credit* at the bank is in doubt. The judge did not *credit* my account of the accident.

3. **accredit** means "to give credit to," "to certify," "to believe." Our institution is *accredited* by the state board of education.

4. **discredit** means "not to believe," "not to accept." Your action is a *discredit* to you and to your family. The prosecutor *discredited* everything the witness said.

Other words built upon the root *cred-* are creditable, creditor, credible, credulous, credibility, incredulous, incredible, and incredibility. You can guess the meanings of these words, but if you are in any doubt, look in your dictionary.

5. dict-

The root *dict-* means "to speak," "to say."

1. **diction** means "the style of speaking or writing dependent upon a choice of words." The speaker was noted for his excellent *diction*. *Diction* varies from region to region in this country.

2. **dictum** means "a saying," "an assertion," "a maxim," "a pronouncement." The governor's *dictum* stopped the riot. There are many *dictums* (or *dicta*) in *Poor Richard's Almanac*.

3. **edict** means "a decree," "a proclamation," "a command." The queen issued an *edict* banning public gatherings. A sovereign's *edict* cannot be ignored.

4. **contradict** means "to deny," "to speak contrary to a statement," "to refute." His actions *contradict* his principles. The witness *contradicted* her earlier testimony.

34

5. **dictate** means "to say or read aloud," "to command with authority." She will *dictate* many letters today. Congress *dictated* changes in the income tax laws.

Other words involving *dict-* are addict, predict, contradictory, dictation, dictionary, dictatorial, predictable, Dictaphone, dictatorship.

QUIZ 10

List at least three words containing each of the following roots. Words in parentheses give keys to root meanings.

1. ag-, act- (do, drive)
2. aud-, audi- (hear)
3. aut-, auto- (self)
4. clam-, claim- (shout)
5. cord- (heart)
6. cumb-, cub- (lie down)
7. duc-, duct- (lead)
8. equ- (equal, even)
9. firm- (strong)
10. gam- (marriage)

QUIZ 11

List at least three words built on each of the following roots. (Clues to meaning appear in parentheses.)

1. ge-, geo- (earth)
2. grat- (pleasing, thankful)
3. junct-, join- (join)
4. leg-, lig-, lect- (choose)
5. mon-, monit- (warn, advise)
6. mov-, mot- (move)
7. nasc-, nat- (to be born)
8. pel-, puls- (to push, to drive)
9. pet-, petit- (to seek, to strive)
10. pon-, pos- (to place, to put)

35

QUIZ 12

Using as guides the clues to meaning given in parentheses, name at least three words formed from each of the following roots:

1. sed-, sid-, sess- (to sit, settle)
2. spec-, spic- (to look)
3. tang-, tact- (to touch)
4. vers-, vert- (to turn)
5. vid-, vis- (to see)

6. volv-, volut- (to roll)
7. cent- (one hundred)
8. doc-, doct- (to teach)
9. flect-, flex- (to bend)
10. her-, hes- (to stick)

QUIZ 13

Each of these words has a different root. What are the roots?

1. discern
2. digest
3. absent
4. precinct
5. intramural

6. posterity
7. biology
8. fluent
9. patient
10. calorie

6

Roots II

This chapter presents five more important building blocks.

6. fac-

This Latin root means "to make," "to do." Also spelled *fic-*, *fact-*, and *fect-*, this root is probably the most widely used of all roots in English.

1. **manufacture** comes from *fact-*, the Latin root *manu-* (meaning "hand"), and the suffix *-ure*. Originally, *manufacture* meant "making by hand" but has come to mean the making of goods and products by machinery or manual labor. *Manufacture* also means "to invent," "to make up," "to fabricate." Sewing machines are *manufactured* in that building. He was driving too fast and had to *manufacture* an excuse for the accident.

2. **fiction** means "something imagined, invented, or feigned." The word is usually applied to "made-up" novels, plays, stories, and narrative poems. In this sense it means "not real," "imaginary." Is this book considered fact or *fiction*? Your explanation for the mistake is pure *fiction*.

3. **factitious** means "artificial," "contrived," "not spontaneous or natural." Her report of activities seems *factitious* to me.

4. **facile** means "easily done," "unconstrained," "affable," "agreeable." His ideas seem weak to me, but he is a *facile* speaker. *Facile* people are pleasant but often boring.

5. **infect** means "to contaminate," "to affect with a disease," "to influence." The enemy tried to *infect* the air with poison gas. His good humor *infected* the audience.

These are among the many words built on this root: affect, effect, facility, fictional, infectious, infection, efficient, affection, proficiency, factual, factor, defect, defection, factory, perfect, defective.

7. fer-

This root means "to carry," "to bring." It appears in scores of words, among them:

1. **transfer,** from the Latin *trans-* ("across") and *fer-*, means "to move from one place to another," "to cause to pass from one person to another." He will have to *transfer* his office from Chicago to Atlanta. Please *transfer* your ownership of the car to your husband.

2. **conference** means "a meeting for discussion," "a bringing together for consultation." The *conference* of executives is scheduled for next Thursday.

3. **fertile** means "capable of bearing and producing," "bringing to life," "productive." This is *fertile* soil. You have a *fertile* imagination.

4. **differ** comes from the Latin *dif-* ("apart") and *fer-*. The word means "to disagree," "to be at variance with." Do you always have to *differ* with my ideas?

5. **offer** comes from a Latin prefix meaning "before" and -*fer*. "To offer" is to present for acceptance or rejection, "to proffer." An *offer* is something proposed or presented. I'd like to *offer* a proposal. Our *offer* for the house was not accepted.

Other words formed from this root include confer, offering, transferable, suffer, preference, referendum, offertory, defer, prefer, refer, reference.

8. gen-

The root *gen-* has several applications but usually appears in words meaning "to give birth to," "to produce," "to cause."

1. **genesis** means "an origin," "creation," "beginning." *Genesis,* the first book in the Bible, gives a story of creation. What was the *genesis* of your fear of the dark?
2. **generate** means "to cause to be," "to bring into existence," "to reproduce." This dynamo *generates* electricity for most of that end of town. Our professor *generates* one idea after another.
3. **homogenize** means "to bring into being by blending unlike elements," "to make parts of the same kind." Dairymen *homogenize* milk by breaking up fat globules.
4. **genocide** means "the extermination of a racial or national group." The word is formed from *gen-* ("race") and -*cide* ("killer"). Hitler's efforts at *genocide* eventually met with disaster.
5. **genital** comes from *genit-* ("to give birth to") and the suffix -*al* ("pertaining to"). *Genital* means "pertaining to the sexual organs and birth-giving processes." That physician specializes in *genital* disorders.

Study your dictionary until you have mastered these additional words built on the root *gen-*: oxygen, hydrogen, ingenious, ingenuity, congenital, genuine, congenial, ingenuous, genial, progenitor.

9. grav-

This Latin root means "heavy," "weighty."

1. **gravity** comes from *grav-* and a suffix meaning "the state or quality of." *Gravity* suggests both "heaviness" and "the force of attraction by which terrestrial bodies tend to fall toward the center of the earth." Don't you feel the force of *gravity* from this height?

2. **grave** means "serious," "weighty," "important," and "critical." She is suffering from a *grave* illness. This *grave* problem must be settled in court. The expression on your face is *grave*.

3. **gravamen** means the part of an accusation that weighs most heavily against the accused, and a grievance. The essential part of this *gravamen* is based on a lie. Why not take the *gravamen* that has arisen to a court of law?

4. **aggravate** means "to make worse," "to make more of a burden or trouble." His anxiety was *aggravated* by a heavy cold.

5. **gravitate** means "to move in response to gravity," "to sink," "to move downward." It also means "to be attracted to," as if by force. The boy and girl quickly *gravitated* toward each other.

10. jac-

This root means "to throw," "to be thrown down."
The root is also spelled *"ject."*

1. **reject** means "to refuse to accept, recognize, or make use of." It also means "to deny," "to refuse to consider," and "to throw away." The machine will *reject* faulty tokens. If you wish to marry you had better not *reject* every proposal you get.

2. **trajectory** means "the path of a moving body," and, in geometry, means a curve that cuts all of a family of surfaces at the same angle. Literally, the word means "to throw across," from *trans-* ("across") and *ject-* ("throw"). What is the *trajectory* of that shooting star?

3. **inject** means "to place, throw, or shoot something into something else." It also means "to introduce." The nurse *injected* morphine into the arm of the victim. The senator *injected* some irony into his remarks.

4. **project** means "to throw forward," "to put forth," "to hurl," "to impel." Try to *project* your voice to the rear of the auditorium. As a noun, *project* means "a plan," "something proposed." The city fathers approved the *project*.

5. **projector** refers to "a machine for throwing an image onto a screen," "a device for projecting a beam of light," and "someone who devises plans." We'll see the whole movie when the *projector* is repaired. Who was the *projector* of that idea?

Other words built on this root are: adjective, projection, abject, dejection, interjection, projectile, object, projectionist, subject, ejaculate, adjacent.

abject — brought low in condition
or status
2. being of the most miserable
kind; wretched

adjacent [ə'dʒeısənt] — close to,
lying near

7

ROOTS III

Here is a discussion of five additional roots and words formed from them.

11. loqu-

This Latin root, also appearing as *loc-* and *locut-*, means "to speak," "to utter."

1. **loquacious** means "talkative," "garrulous," "verbose," "glib." The elderly men in front of the town hall are a *loquacious* lot.

2. **ventriloquist** applies to a person who can originate speech and other sounds so that they appear to come from a source other than the speaker. It is made up of Latin *ventri-* and *loqu-* plus the suffix *-ist*. Literally, the word means "belly speaker." This popular *ventriloquist* uses a wooden dummy.

3. **colloquial** comes from *col-* ("together"), *loqui-* ("to speak"), and *ial* ("pertaining to"). The word means "informal," since it applies to people speaking together in conversational style. The speaker talked in a *colloquial* style.

Some *colloquialisms* are not suitable for formal writing.

4. **elocution** refers to a person's manner of speaking and also to the practice and study of oral speech. It is closely related to *eloquent,* which means "speaking out fully," "speaking fluently and gracefully." The minister is an *eloquent* speaker. Perhaps he studied *elocution* in college.

5. **interlocutor** means "a partner in a dialogue," "a performer in a minstrel show." The judge acted as an *interlocutor* as he tried to get facts from all the witnesses.

12. mit-

Mit- and its variant, *miss-,* mean "to send," "to let go."

1. **commit** literally means "to send together," but in everyday use it means "to perform," "to place in trust," and "to consign." Please *commit* these instructions to memory. The document was *committed* to the fire.

2. **omit** literally means "to send toward," but is used to mean "fail to include," "to leave out something," "to let go." Don't *omit* bacon from your shopping list. By mistake I *omitted* a word from the sentence.

3. **missile** means "something that can be let go," "be sent," and can be applied to a rock, a snowball, an arrow, a bullet, or a rocket. Do you remember the name of the first manned *missile?*

4. **missionary** means "one who is sent on a mission, usually to do charitable, religious, or medical work." Her parents were *missionaries* in China.

5. **permit** means "to send" or "let something go through" and has current meanings of "allow," "consent to," and "authorize." He has a learner's *permit*. No standing or parking is *permitted* on this street.

Other words built on a *mit-, miss-* root include emit, dismiss, omission, transmit, transmitted, transmission, remit, remission, missive, intermittent, emissary.

13. pend-

This root, also appearing as *pens-*, has various meanings: "to hang," "to pay," "to weigh."

1. **suspend** comes from the prefix *sus-* ("under") and *pens-* ("to hang"). Literally meaning "to hang under," *suspend* is now used to mean "to defer action or plans," "to deny a privilege," "to hang from a support." We will have to *suspend* payments on the mortgage. The lantern is *suspended* from a tree limb.
2. **pensive** means "engaged in deep thought," "suspended in troubled revery." *Pensive* persons always weigh their problems seriously.
3. **pendulum** refers to a mass hung from a fixed support and to something that swings back and forth from one course or one idea or opinion. The *pendulum* of public opinion is often difficult to follow.
4. **depend** originally meant "to hang down" but now means "to rely on," "to trust," "to be assured." I'll have to *depend* on you for a place to stay. Our picnic plans *depend* on the weather.
5. **append** means "to add as a supplement," "to attach," "to fix to." He *appended* a codicil to his will. I'd like to *append* a note to your letter.

Other *pend-, pens-* words: appendage, appendant, suspenders, dependable, dependence, dispense, recompense, suspense, indispensable, dispensary, expendable, expenditure, compensate, compensation, pendulous, pending.

44

14. ple-, plet-

This root, in both spellings, means "to fill."

1. **complete** means "filled thoroughly," "full," "entire," "whole," "having all necessary parts." She ran the *complete* course. I have *completed* all the books on that shelf.
2. **replete** literally means "filled again" and is used to mean "plentifully supplied," "abounding," "filled to satiation." After that huge meal I feel *replete*. This menu is *replete* with all necessary vitamins.
3. **deplete** comes from a Latin prefix meaning "not" and *plet-*. The word means "not to fill" and is used to mean "lessening by use or waste," "to use up." If you don't stop spending you will soon *deplete* your funds. My sister's strength was *depleted* by fever.
4. **plethora** means "superabundant," "filled up," "an excess." You will soon receive a *plethora* of advice. No one ever has a *plethora* of love or money.
5. **plenitude** means "abundance," "the condition of being full, ample, or complete." The table was laden with a *plenitude* of rich foods.

Other *ple-, plet-* words: implement, depletion, plenteous, implementation, plenty, plenary, plentiful.

15. port-

The root *port-* means "to carry."

1. **portable** comes from *port-* and the suffix *-able*, meaning "capable of doing and being." *Portable* refers to something that is capable of being moved or carried. She bought a *portable* television set. This lightweight canoe is easily *portable*.

2. **portage** means "the carrying of supplies and boats overland between two waterways," "a route or track by which carrying is done," and "to transport by portage." The *portage* above the falls extends for 200 yards. You will need to *portage* food for a three-week stay.

3. **transportation** means "the act of carrying or conveying from one place to another." It also means "a conveyance," "a means of transport." All buses are in the *transportation* business.

4. **export** comes from the prefix *ex,* meaning "out," and *port-.* *Export* means "to send or carry abroad, especially for sale or trade." This country *exports* much grain to Asia. What is the major *export* of Chile?

5. **import** comes from the Latin prefix *im-* ("in") and *port-.* *Import* means "to bring or carry in from an outside source." A major *import* of this country is natural rubber. Russia seems to need to *import* grain every year.

Other *port-* words include report, portal, deport, deportee, transport, disport, porter, support, reporter, supporter.

8
Roots IV

Here is a discussion of words formed from these roots: *rupt-*, *scrib-*, *tract-*, *vent-*, and *voc-*. In addition to the twenty-five words singled out for special attention in this chapter, note carefully the words used in explanation of them. Also, look up these five roots in your dictionary and find still more words that are built from them.

16. rupt-

This root means "to break," "to burst."

1. **disrupt** comes from the prefix *dis-* ("apart") and *rupt-*. The word means not only "to break," "to burst," but also "to throw into confusion," "to upset the order of." The hecklers *disrupted* the scheduled meeting. A serious accident *disrupted* our plans for the trip.
2. **abrupt** means "sudden," "unexpectedly," "cut or broken off short." Your comments are both rude and *abrupt*.
3. **interrupt** means "to break the uniformity or continuity of some action," "to hinder or stop something," "to break

in upon some act or speech." The movie was *interrupted* when the film broke. Our plans were *interrupted* by a shortage of money.

4. **erupt** means "to force out," "to release suddenly," "to explode," "to become violently active." That volcano will soon *erupt*. The meeting *erupted* into a near riot.

5. **rupture,** as a verb, means "to break apart or break open." As a noun, *rupture* means "a bursting," "a breaking." Bankruptcy *ruptured* all our plans. The *rupture* between Syria and Israel was serious.

Other *rupt-* words include eruption, corrupt, corruption, disruption, and disruptive.

17. scrib-

This root, which also appears as *script-,* means "to write."

1. **manuscript** means "a book, document, or other composition written by hand." Although *manuscript* literally means "handwritten," it is commonly used to refer to copy (material) submitted for printing or other use whether the copy is handwritten or typewritten. Your *manuscript* is neatly typed. The author lost his *manuscript* on a bus.

2. **inscription** means "the wording on a coin or medal," "an epitaph," "the dedication of a book or other work of art." The *inscription* on her tombstone is "She kept the faith."

3. **prescribe** is built on *scribe-* and the prefix *pre-*. The word has more than one meaning: to set down as a rule; to order or ordain; to recommend a treatment or remedy; to establish rules or regulations. The physician *prescribed* no remedies for my uncle. The *prescribed* dress for the party is "formal."

4. **describe** is introduced by the prefix *de-* (meaning "down"). It is used to mean "to give an account of some action," "to transmit an image or impression," and "to trace or draw." When you *describe* someone you write down or speak words that draw a picture. The teacher told us to *describe* a typical classroom.

5. **subscribe** comes from word elements meaning "to write beneath." It is used to mean "to sign," "to pledge or contribute," "to express approval or consent." I do not *subscribe* to your proposal. Why do you *subscribe* to that magazine?

Other *scribe-, script-* words are transcribe, inscribe, prescribe, ascribe, conscript, conscription, circumscribe, scribble, Scripture, and script.

18. tract-

This root means "to pull," "to draw," "to drag."

1. **tractable** means "easily managed or controlled," "not difficult to pull or drag into line," "easily handled or worked." Her favorite horse is unusually *tractable*. Most good medical students are *tractable*.

2. **extract** literally means "to pull out," but it has several associated meanings: to draw forth forcibly; to obtain despite resistance; to remove for consideration or study; to copy a passage from a book or other source. This machine *extracts* syrup from cane. An exodontist is a dentist who *extracts* teeth. Please read me that *extract* again. The cake tasted of vanilla *extract*.

3. **detract** means "to diminish," "to take a desirable part of." Your clothes *detract* from your chances for a job. Loud talk by others *detracted* from our enjoyment of the play.

4. **contract** (to draw together) means "to establish or settle by agreement," "to shrink," "to shorten," and, as a noun, means "an agreement," "a paper or document detailing an agreement." The *contract* is fair and complete. The medicine made the pupils of his eyes seem to *contract*.
5. **distract** literally means "to draw away" and is regularly used to mean "to bewilder," "to confuse," "to divert mind or attention." Don't let your love for him *distract* you. Noises from the pneumatic drill *distracted* the listeners at the musical.

Other *tract-* words: tractor, extraction, attraction, attractive, contraction, contractor, contractual, detractor, distraction, extraction, protract, retract, tract, traction, subtract, subtraction.

19. ven-

This root, which also appears as *vent-*, means "to come," "to move toward."

1. **event,** which literally means "to come out," "to happen" is used for "an occurrence, experience, or incident." *Event* also means the actual outcome or final result of something and "one of the items in a program of entertainment or sports." The election of 1800 was an important *event*. My solo was the last *event* on the program.
2. **convention** means "a coming together," "an assembly," "an agreement dealing with a specific subject," "a device or technique." This *convention* was well attended. There are many *conventions* for the treatment of prisoners of war.
3. **revenue** means "a collection of funds," "the yield from property," "the income of a government." This state collects millions of dollars of *revenue* from sales taxes.

50

4. **circumvent** means "to get around something," "to come around," "to overcome," "to avoid." We tried to *circumvent* the parking regulations. Take some aspirin and *circumvent* a cold.
5. **intervene** means "to come between," "to appear to lie between two things," "to hinder," "to modify." The referee *intervened* in the players' fight. Please don't try to *intervene* in our dispute.

Other *ven-, vent-* words: invent, prevent, prevention, preventive, advent, adventure, venturesome, venture, inventive, inventor, eventful, eventuality, eventual, convenient, convenience, conventional, unconventional.

20. voc-

This Latin root (also appearing as *vok-* and *voke-*) means both "voice" and "to call."

1. **vocal** means of or pertaining to the voice; having a voice capable of emitting sound; resounding with speech. The crew's displeasure was both physical and *vocal*. He was *vocal* in favor of his friend.
2. **invoke** means "to call upon for help," "to appeal to," "to petition." The defendant *invoked* the Fifth Amendment. The rabbi *invoked* God's blessing on the assembly.
3. **vociferous** means "making an outcry," "clamorous," "characterized by loudness." The mob was *vociferous* in its demands.
4. **vocation** means "a calling," "an urge to undertake a line of work to which one feels called," "an occupation or profession." His law practice is his *vocation*, but his avocation is gardening.
5. **revoke** means "to recall," "to annul or avoid by recall-

ing," "to fail to follow suit." Our leader *revoked* her permission for us to leave. When I *revoked* during the bridge game my partner was furious.

Other *voc-, vok-, voke-* words: evoke, vocalist, vocalize, vociferate, vocabulary, provoke, provocation, provocative, irrevocable, revocation.

9
Combining Forms

A *combining form* is a word element that combines other words, or parts of words, to form compounds. Examples are "logy" as in *psychology,* "micro" as in *microscope,* and "Sine" as in *Sinophile* (one friendly to the Chinese) or *Sino-Tibetan. Graph,* for example, although it is a word by itself, appears frequently as a combining form in such words as "photography," "geography," and "lithography."

Experts differ in the ways in which they classify combining forms, prefixes, roots, and suffixes. What one writer on language would call a root, another would term a prefix or combining form or suffix. Even so, knowing the meanings and applications of forms like the following, however you choose to call them, will greatly increase your vocabulary.

1. **anima** means "life," "breath."
animation	animate	animalism
animal	inanimate	animadvert

2. **aqua** means "water."
aquarium	aquacade	aquifer
aqueduct	aquamarine	aqualung

53

3. **bios** means "life."

biopsy	bioplasm	biometrics
bionics	biosphere	biosynthesis

4. **culpa** means "fault," "negligence."

culprit	culpability	culpableness
culpable	culpably	culpatory

5. **domus** means "house," "home."

domicile	domesticate	domesticity
domestic	domesticable	domestication

6. **ego** means "I."

egoism	egocentric	egomania
egotism	egoist	egotist

7. **facilis** means "easy."

facile	facilitate	facilitation
facility	facilely	facileness

8. **gramma** means "letter."

grammar	grammarian	grammalogue
grammatical	grammarless	grammaticism

9. **lex** means "law."

lawyer	lawful	lawmaker
legal	lawless	legality

10. **liber** means "book."

library	libretti	librarian
libretto	libriform	librettist

11. **locus** means "place."

locality	location	locate
local	locator	locative

12. **navis** means "ship."

navigate	navy	navigation
naval	navigable	navigator

13. **opus** means "work."

operation	operational	operative
opera	operate	operator

14. **populus** means "people."

population   populace   populate

popularity   populous   popularize

15. **sanctus** means "holy."

sanctuary   sanctity   sanctimonious

sanctify   sanctifier   sanction

16. **sophia** means "wisdom."

sophisticated   sophism   sophomore

sophistry   philosophy   sophist

17. **spectro** means "light."

spectrum   spectroscope   spectrogram

spectroscopy   spectroscopic   spectrograph

18. **tactus** means "quiet," "silence."

tacit   taciturnly   tacitly

taciturn   taciturnity   tacitness

19. **thermo** means "heat."

thermometer   thermal   thermochemistry

thermostat   isotherm   thermodynamics

20. **vita** means "life."

vitamin   vitality   vitals

vital   vitalize   vitally

QUIZ 14

Give the meaning of each of these combining forms.
Then use each form in a sentence.

1. aristos   5. hostis   9. plus,
2. beatus   6. mater   pluris
3. causa   7. pedi   10. umbra
4. decem   8. petra

QUIZ 15

Match each numbered word ending (suffix or combining form) with the proper key word. For example: "2. -arch" is matched with "E. ruler" as in "monarch."

1.	-androus	A.	inferior
2.	-arch	B.	male
3.	-ase	C.	ancient
4.	-aster	D.	decomposes
		E.	ruler

5.	-cephalic	A.	head
6.	-cide	B.	tree
7.	-cracy	C.	rule
8.	-dendron	D.	kill
		E.	judge

9.	-dom	A.	becoming
10.	-esce	B.	realm
11.	-ese	C.	guilty
12.	-fold	D.	times
		E.	dialect

13.	-gamy	A.	woman
14.	-gen	B.	walking
15.	-grade	C.	producing
16.	-gyny	D.	union
		E.	evaluation

17.	-hippus	A.	medicine
18.	-hood	B.	shelter

19. -iatry	C. whole group
20. -kin	D. horse
	E. little

21. -lent	A. slender
22. -ling	B. full
23. -lith	C. speaking
24. -logue	D. little
	E. stone

QUIZ 16

For each numbered word ending follow directions given in the preceding quiz.

25. -lysis	A. shape
26. -mancy	B. dissolving
27. -morph	C. divination
28. -ode	D. path
	E. infesting

29. -oid	A. colored
30. -pathic	B. eating
31. -petal	C. moving toward
32. -phage	D. suffering
	E. resembling

33. -phile	A. fear
34. -phobe	B. plant
35. -phyte	C. liking
36. -pod	D. foot
	E. watery

37.	-pter	A.	condition of
38.	-ship	B.	tending toward, like
39.	-some	C.	wing
40.	-stat	D.	holding steady
		E.	excessive

41.	-ster	A.	turning toward
42.	-tomy	B.	person who
43.	-trope	C.	little
44.	-ule	D.	crime
		E.	cutting

45.	-dont	A.	manner
46.	-vorous	B.	fatigued
47.	-wise	C.	tooth
48.	-ard	D.	excess
		E.	feeding on

10

Prefixes I

A *prefix* is a letter or group of letters (called an ''affix'') placed before a root, other prefix, or word. The addition of a prefix to a root or word alters meaning and is a common and frequent way of adding words to the vocabulary.

The word *prefix* comes from two Latin words meaning ''to attach or place before.'' Prefixes can be difficult and even tricky to handle because (1) the same prefix may have more than one spelling; (2) the exact meaning of all prefixes is not fully clear; (3) some prefixes (such as *graph-* and *bene-*) are also thought of as roots. Even so, prefixes are next to roots in importance in building a vocabulary.

Learning the meanings of the prefixes explained in this chapter and the next will add greatly to your instant recognition of the meanings of words when you hear or read them.

1. **ab-** *(abs-)* means ''from,'' ''off,'' ''away.'' It appears in a word like *abnormal,* which means ''not normal, not average, not typical, away from normalcy.'' Other *abs-, ab-* words:

absent	abscess	abduct

absolve	abuse	absorb
absolute	abort	

2. **ad-** means "to," "toward," "at," "near," "against."

advice	adhere	admire
adverse	adjective	addict
address	adapt	

3. **ante-** means "in front of," "before."

anteroom	antechamber	antecedent
antedate	antebellum	antediluvian
antecede	antecessor	

4. **anti-** means "against," "opposed to."

antisocial	antipathy	antiseptic
antiwar	antibiotic	antifreeze
antidote	anticlimax	

5. **bi-** means "twice," "doubly," "two."

bicycle	bilingual	binomial
bifocal	bigamy	bilateral
bipartisan	biannual	

6. **circum-** means "about," "around," "on all sides."

circumference	circumvent	circumnavigate
circumflex	circumstance	circumlocution
circumscribe	circumspect	

7. **com-** (also spelled *col-, con-,* and *cor-*) means "to-gether," "with," "completely."

combat	coerce	coexist
compatriot	concede	correlate
collaborate	collide	

8. **contra-** (also *counter-*) means "opposing," "opposite," "contrary," "against."

contradict	counterfeit	counterbalance
contraception	countersign	contradistinction
contraband	counterattack	

9. **de-** means "down," "away," "off."

declare	detract	degrade

deform   defend   decrease
descend   demerit

10. **dis-** *(di-, dif-)* means "apart," "away from," "not."
dislocate   disability   disloyal
disconnect   disable   difference
disarm   divert

11. **ex-** (also *e, ef-*) means "out," "out of," "from," "former."
exclude   excavate   efface
effervesce   evade   exhale
exhume   evolve

12. **extra-** means "outside of," "beyond."
extraordinary   extralegal   extrapolate
extracurricular extrasensory   extramural
extramarital   extraneous

13. **hyper-** means "over," "excessive."
hyperbole   hypercorrect   hyperbolic
hypercritical   hyperconscious hypersensitive
hyperacidity   hyperactive

14. **hypo-** means "under," "beneath."
hypodermic   hypoglycemia   hypothesis
hypochondriac   hypotenuse   hypostasis
hypothetical   hypothecate

15. **in-** (also spelled *em-, en, il, im-*) means "not," "without," and "into," "in."
indefinite   embrace   indemnity
enclose   impossible   invalidate
illogical   illiterate

16. **inter-** means "between," "among," "with each other."
intercollegiate interfere   intercontinental
interdependent intercept   intercede
interject   interbreed

17. **ir-** is a variant of *in-* and has identical meanings.
irregular   irreparable   irreligious

| irresolute | irrespective | irresistible |
| irrelevant | irresponsible | |

18. **intra-** means "inside," "within."

intravenous	intramolecular	intrauterine
intranuclear	intraorbital	intravascular
intramuscular	intrastate	

19. **mal-** *(male-)* means "evil," "wrong," "bad."

malady	malaria	malediction
malcontent	malfeasance	malignant
malodorous	maladroit	

20. **mis-** is a variant of *mal-* and has the meanings of that prefix as well as "wrongness" and "badness."

misadventure	mislead	misanthrope
miscreant	misrepresent	mistake
misbehave	misspell	

QUIZ 17

Many words, roots, and prefixes from Greek and Latin are used in numbering, counting, and measuring. Do you recall that September, October, November, and December are so-called because they are the seventh, eighth, ninth, and tenth months of the old Roman calendar? Study this brief chart:

	GREEK	LATIN
one	mono (monogamous)	uni (union)
first	proto (prototype)	prim (primary)
three	tri (tricycle)	tri (trio)
four	tetra (tetrameter)	quatr (quadruped, quarter)
five	penta (pentagon)	quint (quintet)

Now look up the Greek and Latin origins of *two*, *six*, *seven*, *eight*, *nine*, *ten*, and *half*.

QUIZ 18

Recall the meaning of the following prefixes and then list five common words containing each prefix.

bi-   pre-
cross-   non-   sub-

QUIZ 19

Name two words beginning with each of these prefixes:

1. a- (not)
2. ambi- (around, both)
3. audio- (hearing)
4. bio- (life)
5. col- (together)
6. en-, em- (in, on)
7. epi- (upon, before)
8. hemi- (half)
9. il- (not)
10. neo- (new)
11. para- (beside)
12. peri- (beyond)
13. pseudo- (false)
14. ultra- (in excess of)
15. un- (not)

QUIZ 20

For each of the following prefixes or roots, state first its meaning and then list a word containing that prefix or root.

1. hypo-
2. intra-
3. syn-, sym-
4. hetero-
5. homo- (Greek meaning)
6. ortho-

7. omni-
8. dyn-
9. reg-
10. urb-
11. cosm-
12. phil-
13. phob-

14. fid-
15. cred-
16. duc-
17. turb-
18. rupt-
19. ben-, bon-
20. mal-

11
Prefixes II

Here are twenty more prefixes with listings of words they begin. Knowing the meaning of a prefix will not guarantee your knowing the meaning of the word it introduces. But understanding the meaning of a prefix *and* the root that follows will establish the term in your recognition and active vocabularies.

21. **mono-** means "one," "single," "alone."

monopoly	monogamy	monody	monochrome
monotone	monologue	monolith	monogram

22. **multi-** means "much," "more than one," "many."

multigraph	multicolored	multiplication	multifarious
multiform	multiplicity	multiple	multipartite

23. **non-** means "not."

nonsense	nonconformist	nonrestrictive
nonplus	nonexistent	nondescript
nonchalant	nonentity	

24. **ob-,** a prefix the spelling of which changes to *oc-, of-,* or *op-* depending on the letter that follows, means "over," "against," "inverse shape or attachment."

object   occupy   offend   oppress
obstacle   occlude   opponent   offensive

25. **out-** means ''located outside'' and ''to a surprising degree.''

outside   outfield   outcast   outcome
outlet   outgrow   outstanding   outdistance

26. **over-** means ''location above,'' ''superiority of rank,'' ''movement above or below a position.''

overage   oversee   oversight   overbid
overbear   overweight   overwrought   overburden

27. **per-** means ''through,'' ''by,'' ''around,'' ''wrongly.''

perimeter   permeate   percent   percussion
perjury   perpendicular percolate   perfect

28. **poly-** means ''many,'' ''more than one,'' ''much.''

polygamy   polyglot   polygraph
polygon   polytheism   polysynthetic
polysyllable   polychromatic

29. **post-** means ''after,'' ''behind.''

postpone   postwar   postgraduate postdate
posterity   postscript   posthumous   posterior

30. **pre-** means ''preceding,'' ''prior to,'' ''before.''

prerequisite precocious precipitate precept
premeditate precinct   precipice   presume

31. **pro-** means ''before,'' ''forward,'' ''in place of,'' ''forth.''

pronoun   profane   proceed   professor
procession   profess   production proclaim

32. **re-** means ''back,'' ''again.''

recall   rebel   regenerate   refresh
rebuff   receive   recession   return

33. **retro-** means ''backward,'' ''back,'' ''situated behind.''

retrograde   retrogress   retroactive   retrovert
retrospect   retroflex   retrocede   retrorocket

34. **se-** means ''away,'' ''apart,'' ''aside,'' ''without.''

| secede | seduce | select | segregate |
| secure | security | seclude | sedition |

35. **sub-** means "under," "beneath," "below."

| subway | subsidy | subscribe | subtraction |
| subcutaneous | subconscious | submarine | subordinate |

36. **super-** means "above," "over," "greater than."

superfluous	superstition	superintendent
supernatural	superficial	supercilious
supersede	supervise	

37. **sym-** (also appearing as *syl-* and *syn-*) means "with," "together with."

| sympathy | symphony | syncope | syndicate |
| syllable | symmetry | synonym | synthesis |

38. **tele-** indicates "distance," "afar."

television	telepathy	telecommunication
telephone	telescope	televise
telegraph	telecast	

39. **trans-** means "across," "over," "beyond," "on the other side of."

| transatlantic | transfuse | transaction | transport |
| transfer | transitory | transgress | transmit |

40. **uni-** means "single," "only one."

| unify | union | unison | Unitarian |
| unique | unilateral | universal | uniform |

12
Suffixes I

A *suffix* is something added to something else. In word study, a suffix is a building block added at the end of a root or word after the primary meaning of that term has been established.

The meaning of many suffixes is general. A suffix does not so much change the meaning of a word to which it is attached as it changes the *use* of that word (its function, its part of speech). A suffix will often indicate whether a word is used as the name of a person, place, or item (that is, as a *noun*); as an action word (a *verb*); or as a modifier (an *adjective* or *adverb*). A suffix can also indicate the *number* (singular or plural) of nouns and verbs as well as the *tense* of verbs.

Although not as helpful in building a vocabulary as knowing about prefixes, some knowledge of suffixes will help. This knowledge is particularly useful with such suffixes as *-graph, -scope,* and *-meter,* which are not only words but may also be considered as roots or combining forms.

The element *-graph* can mean "a writing or drawing" and "an instrument for making sounds or writing." A *phonograph* is a sound-producing machine. *Telegraph* means "long distance writing," a device using impulses sent by wire or radio waves. An *autograph* is one's own signature.

The suffix *-scope*, meaning "an instrument for seeing, observing," appears in such words as *microscope*, *telescope*, and *stethoscope*.

The suffix *-meter* means "an instrument for measuring" and "a measure." It is used in such words as *thermometer*, *diameter*, and *speedometer*.

Verb-forming Suffixes

Here are a half dozen suffixes that form verbs or that indicate the tenses of a verb:

1. **-fy**

   | gratify | mollify | modify |
   | justify | falsify | electrify |

2. **-ish**

   | extinguish | demolish | finish |
   | diminish | admonish | punish |

3. **-ate**

   | nominate | segregate | terminate |
   | regulate | decimate | gravitate |

4. **-ize**

   | criticize | minimize | aggrandize |
   | terrorize | localize | pasteurize |

5. **-ed**

   | talk—talked | hang—hanged | ask—asked |
   | knit—knitted | attack—attacked | swell—swelled |

6. **-ing**

   | drive—driving | spring—springing | steal—stealing |
   | throw—throwing | sleep—sleeping | cry—crying |

Noun-forming Suffixes

Here are ten suffixes of nouns that mean a follower of; a citizen or native of; a place or instrument for; a person or thing that performs or is characterized by or connected with something:

1. **-ar**
   | scholar | beggar | dollar |
   | cellar | sugar | burglar |

2. **-ary**
   | boundary | auxiliary | secretary |
   | library | dictionary | mortuary |

3. **-hood**
   | childhood | statehood | womanhood |
   | falsehood | likelihood | boyhood |

4. **-ician**
   | magician | electrician | politician |
   | pediatrician | logician | optician |

5. **-ics**
   | fanatics | politics | semantics |
   | dramatics | optics | linguistics |

6. **-ist**
   | pharmacist | druggist | genealogist |
   | communist | optometrist | podiatrist |

7. **-ite**
   | termite | socialite | suburbanite |
   | respite | Mennonite | cosmopolite |

8. **ory**
   | lavatory | rectory | dormitory |
   | history | story | directory |

9. **-polis**
   | metropolis | Annapolis | cosmopolis |
   | cosmopolitan | Indianapolis | metropolitan |

10. **-ship**

friendship	salesmanship	fellowship
statesmanship	comradeship	partnership

So much for verb-forming and noun-forming suffixes. In the next chapter you will find out about suffixes that form modifiers (adjectives and adverbs).

QUIZ 21

Scores of words end in these suffixes. How many can you name?

-ary	-cide
-gram	-eer
-proof	-work

QUIZ 22

State the general meaning of each of these suffixes and then list five words containing each suffix.

-al	-ist
-est	-ment
-less	

QUIZ 23

Name two words ending in each of these suffixes.

1. -ana
2. -ance
3. -dom
4. -fold

5. -ful
6. -ice

7. -ism
8. -ity

QUIZ 24

State the meaning of each of the following prefixes and suffixes and list five words containing each. Remember, if you're stuck, call on your good friend, the dictionary. This is a review because you have already encountered these items many times in this book.

1. mono-	6. micro-	11. -est	16. -let
2. non-	7. auto-	12. -able	17. -ness
3. pseudo-	8. sub-	13. -ment	18. -like
4. semi-	9. bi-	14. -graph	19. -er
5. over-	10. multi-	15. -ish	20. -ine

13
Suffixes II

Suffixes added to roots or words form many more modifiers than they do nouns or verbs. What follows in this chapter is a discussion of twenty of the most often used suffixes as makers of adjectives and adverbs. Several of them also make nouns and verbs, which were indicated in the preceding chapter.

1. **-able**
   peaceable   breakable   profitable
   acceptable   favorable   comfortable

2. **-acious**
   tenacious   spacious   mendacious
   voracious   loquacious   fallacious

3. **-al**
   postal   equal   inimical
   manual   filial   polemical

4. **-an**
   human   Italian   crustacean
   Grecian   urban   Stygian

5. **-ary**
   secondary   primary   imaginary
   honorary   tertiary   elementary

6. **-ate**

    adequate   affectionate   Italianate
    aggregate   ornate   profligate

7. **-ed**

    educated   overrated   superannuated
    dogged   terrified   scratched

8. **-ent**

    intent   malcontent   prescient
    stringent   content   recumbent

9. **-er**

    smaller   lesser   sooner
    quicker   warmer   greater

10. **-est**

    tallest   smallest   hottest
    earliest   latest   greatest

11. **-ible**

    edible   visible   combustible
    audible   terrible   horrible

12. **-ic**

    academic   exotic   chromatic
    despotic   systematic   pandemic

13. **-id**

    lucid   humid   solid
    gravid   pellucid   stolid

14. **-ile**

    servile   juvenile   facile
    docile   agile   volatile

15. **-ine**

    masculine   feminine   internecine
    canine   bovine   feline

16. **-ing**

    winning   crying   cooking
    jumping   talking   smiling

17. **-ish**

| foolish | waspish | mannish |
| prudish | boyish | girlish |

18. **-less**

| sleepless | noiseless | heartless |
| stainless | lifeless | priceless |

19. **-ly**

| friendly | physically | suddenly |
| quickly | sadly | kindly |

20. **-ory**

| introductory | compulsory | laudatory |
| ambulatory | perfunctory | desultory |

Now that you are aware of suffixes and the roles they play in forming verbs, nouns, adjectives, and adverbs, think of other suffixes and list the words they can form. For example, consider the suffix *-ism*. Words such as *stoicism, skepticism, heroism,* and *alcoholism* should get you started.

See what you can do with sixteen more fairly common suffixes:

-acity	-fic	-mony	-ous
-acy	-ion	-oid	-sis
-ant	-less	-or	-ty
-ence	-ment	-ose	-ure

14

Synonyms

A *synonym* is a word having the same, or nearly the same, meaning as another in the language, such as the words "glad," "elated," and "joyful." A synonym is also an expression or word accepted as another name for something, such as "ship of state" for "government" and "Arcadia" for "pastoral simplicity."

English not only has the largest vocabulary of any language in the world but also the most synonyms. This wealth has been created because English has grown over the centuries by constant borrowing from other languages. For example, when new French words came into use in England after the Norman Conquest (1066), a speaker had a choice of synonyms, such as the French "cure" or Anglo-Saxon "heal." These were other choices:

table—board	mirror—glass
labor—work	power—might
poignant—sharp	assemble—meet
ox—beef	calf—veal
swine—pork	deer—venison
hitting—assault	stealing—larceny
striking—battery	robbing—burglary

Synonyms in English are of many kinds. Some related words, although not exactly similar, have gradations of the same meaning, such as *tip, heel, slant, tilt,* and *list;* or *howl, scream, screech,* and *yammer.*

Another group of synonyms results from outright borrowing:

foreword (English) or preface (French)
introduction (Latin) or prolegomenon (Greek)

Or consider these names for areas of land:

plain (French)	savannah (Spanish)
steppe (Russian)	prairie (French voyageur)
pampas (Spanish)	tundra (Russian)

Actually, there are few, if any, exact synonyms; no precise and complete equivalences of meaning. Certainly there are no two words or expressions that can be interchanged in all the contexts in which either might be used. It's all right to say "I *misplaced* my pencil" and "I *mislaid* my pocketbook." And yet *misplace* can apply to both small and large objects whereas *mislay* applies only to small. It really won't do to say "I *mislaid* my suitcase." That is, words that are synonymous in *one* of their meanings may differ in other meanings.

To distinguish between words of similar, but not always identical, meaning is important for both clear expression and vocabulary growth. Making lists of synonyms and distinguishing among their meanings is an effective way to enlarge your vocabulary. Many dictionaries include listings and explanations of hundreds of synonyms. When looking up a word, carefully study the synonym entries. If you do this, you may be able to choose a more exact and effective word and at the same time enlarge your active vocabulary.

For example, after becoming aware of synonyms, will you have to write that the baby is *cute*, the game *thrilling*, the idea *interesting*, the dress *glamorous* or *chic*, the play *exciting?* A study of synonyms for *old* might add to your vocabulary these words, among others: *immemorial, aged, ancient, aboriginal, decrepit, antique, hoary, elderly, patriarchal, venerable, passé, antiquated, antediluvian.*

With the aid of your dictionary or such standard works as *Roget's International Thesaurus of English Words, Webster's Dictionary of Synonyms, Use the Right Word, Crabb's English Synonyms,* or *Funk and Wagnalls Standard Handbook of Synonyms* you can enrich and increase your word power. These and similar reference books will help you to avoid confusing such "look-alikes" as *disinterested* and *uninterested* or *affect* and *effect.* These sources will provide you with new names and terms for everyday objects, places, and actions. But if you do not have access to any of the other word books, your dictionary will serve very well.

Suppose, for example, that you wish to invite a distinguished person to have a meal. Would you invite him or her to join you at a—

café	diner
eatery	cafeteria
lunch counter	luncheonette
greasy spoon	coffee shop
dining room	coffee house

Each of these words means a place where food and refreshments are provided. But although the words have a shared meaning, the places they indicate differ greatly in atmosphere, quality, and cost.

On the street you see a badly crippled or deformed person begging money. You say to yourself "That's a *pitiful* sight."

You might have used any of these words instead of "pitiful": *wretched, sorrowful, pitiable, piteous, pathetic, miserable, moving.*

If asked, you might say that during the day you have done the *usual* things you do every day. It might more exactly express your meaning to say, instead of "usual," *accustomed, conventional, regular, common, wonted, habitual,* or *customary.*

The idea of "brief existence" can be expressed by many words: *flitting, fleeting, short, temporary, momentary, transient, passing, fugitive, ephemeral, evanescent, flying, transitory, short-lived,* and *impermanent.*

What word applies most clearly to:

     a. One's hesitation in reaching a decision
     b. The life of an insect
     c. A quick glance
     d. A worthless book
     e. A sudden, quickly relieved headache

The answers of twenty-one people who responded to this question varied, but the majority vote was (a) momentary, temporary; (b) fleeting, ephemeral; (c) flitting, flying; (d) short-lived; (e) passing.

• You will find it interesting and fun-producing to search your dictionary for words conveying such different ideas and impressions as:

careful	evil
strong	rude
happy	lewd
smelly	bizarre
pretty	stupid

Make up for yourself further tests involving ideas, person-ality traits, impressions, and characteristics. Your success in de-veloping and completing such tests (call them "games") will add to your pleasure *and* your vocabulary.

QUIZ 25

The word *choice* has numerous synonyms. List at least five.

QUIZ 26

The word *allow* has several synonyms, among them *let, permit, suffer,* and *tolerate*. Name other syn-onyms for *let*.

QUIZ 27

List the synonyms given in your dictionary for each of the following words:

1. street
2. opposite
3. frank
4. answer (verb and noun)
5. trite
6. defame
7. yield
8. magic
9. tolerant
10. effort

15

Antonyms

An *antonym* is a word opposite in meaning to another, as "fast" is the opposite of "slow" and "light" is the opposite of "dark." Strictly speaking, an antonym is a word opposed in meaning to another word that is its equal in range and breadth of application. A true antonym makes invalid everyone of the meanings and implications of another word.

Studying antonyms will contribute to vocabulary growth. For example, seeking antonyms for *praise* may add to your vocabulary such words as *vilify, stigmatize, lampoon, abuse, censure, blame, deprecate, condemn, impugn, denigrate, disparage*, and *inveigh against*. Even such a simple word as *join* has numerous approximate opposites, among them *uncouple, separate, sunder, unyoke, cleave, disconnect*, and *dissever*.

A study of antonyms, however, is not nearly so important in vocabulary building as is attenton to synonyms. Why? Because an antonym, or a list of antonyms, is normally used by a speaker or writer searching for a word rather than a meaning. Also, it should be noted that many words have no precise and exact opposite. There are, for example, some words related to *weird* and *spell* and *advice* but no specific opposites.

Yet antonyms should not be overlooked and entirely ignored. A search for them will help you to avoid overuse of many words that have become flat and stale. For instance, if you wish to express the idea of "artistic" or "tasteful" in opposite fashion, you could resort to:

shoddy	inartistic
tasteless	distasteful
displeasing	repellent
gaudy	unaesthetic

If you need an antonym for "healthy" you can come up with:

ill	diseased	wasted	fragile
sick	emaciated	worn	frail
sickly	failing	delicate	unhealthy

Notice how antonyms for the following words will begin to increase your word hoard:

1. *humane*
    barbaric, cruel, savage, uncouth, brutal, pitiless,
    inhuman, unfeeling, uncivilized, hardhearted, merciless,
    ruthless
2. *idle*
    active, busy, occupied, working, employed, industrious
3. *carry*
    drop, let go, shake off, throw off, throw down, discard
4. *despair*
    cheer, confidence, courage, hopefulness, trust,
    expectation, assurance, anticipation, elation, hope,
    optimism, encouragement
5. *hurt*
    soothe, console, comfort, benefit, aid, solace, condole,
    assuage

6. *favorable*
   doomed, ill-fated, inauspicious, unfavorable, adverse, inimical, hostile, unlucky, incompatible
7. *slow*
   agile, quick, fast, speedy, rapid, lively, brisk, swift, sprightly, spry
8. *faithful*
   fickle, faithless, unfaithful, wavering, untrustworthy, capricious, false, untrue, perfidious, inconstant
9. *injustice*
   equity, fairness, fair play, honesty, impartiality, rectitude, faithfulness, lawfulness, uprightness
10. *opponent*
    friend, associate, companion, crony, intimate, confidant, partner, colleague, ally, co-worker, cohort, accomplice

When consulting your dictionary for a word, never fail to look at the end of the entry. Often you will discover a list of synonyms or antonyms or both. Studying these lists will quickly add to your store of words and enable you to get them into your active vocabulary.

QUIZ 28

With the help of your dictionary (or a thesaurus), list one or more antonyms for each of the following:

1. professional
2. solicitous
3. huge
4. repudiate
5. petty
6. decrease
7. grave
8. sophisticated
9. fine
10. arrogant

16

Test Yourself

Test 1

Match each numbered word with its lettered definition.

1.	Penury	(a)	marked by shrewdness
2.	Deter	(b)	express indirectly
3.	Anticipate	(c)	utter and total confusion
4.	Proficient	(d)	open to view
5.	Instigate	(e)	extreme poverty
6.	Rebate	(f)	take away
7.	Composite	(g)	a return of a portion of a payment
8.	Wrath	(h)	prevent from acting
9.	Dire	(i)	noisy in an offensive manner
10.	Jocular	(j)	urge forward
11.	Adroit	(k)	showing reverence or devotion
12.	Imply	(l)	deserving imitation
13.	Vulnerable	(m)	violent anger
14.	Exemplary	(n)	given to jesting
15.	Pious	(o)	a false idea
16.	Blatant	(p)	foresee

17.	Rescind	(q)	made up of distinct parts
18.	Overt	(r)	desperately urgent
19.	Chaos	(s)	open to attack
20.	Fallacy	(t)	well advanced in an art or occupation

Test 2

From the choices given, select the word that most nearly means the same as the italicized word.

1. *Tepid* most nearly means (a) foreign (b) precise (c) moderately warm (d) intensely interesting (e) hopeless
2. *Profane* most nearly means (a) skillful (b) irreverent (c) competent (d) profound (e) pleasant
3. *Relinquish* most nearly means (a) abandon (b) remain (c) control (d) construct (e) modify
4. *Contrite* most nearly means (a) opposed (b) foolish (c) furious (d) decisive (e) sorry
5. *Hypothesis* most nearly means (a) complexity (b) theory (c) feeling (d) fascination (e) indication
6. *Garnish* most nearly means (a) direct (b) cover (c) frequent (d) embellish (e) complete
7. *Garrulous* most nearly means (a) dangerous (b) angry (c) talkative (d) loud (e) persistent
8. *Patent* most nearly means (a) defective (b) exact (c) quiet (d) careful (e) obvious
9. *Impeccable* most nearly means (a) flawless (b) imperfect (c) inconsiderate (d) competent (e) workable
10. *Fallacious* most nearly means (a) incomplete (b) faltering (c) deceptive (d) resolute (e) aggravating
11. *Nurture* most nearly means (a) object (b) confess (c) foster (d) separate (e) fail
12. *Repugnant* most nearly means (a) acceptable (b) modern (c) adequate (d) dreary (e) repellent

13. *Replica* most nearly means (a) substitute (b) reproduction (c) remembrance (d) movement (e) strategy
14. *Contrived* most nearly means (a) controlled (b) destroyed (c) artificial (d) incomplete (e) convincing
15. *Remunerate* most nearly means (a) pay (b) enumerate (c) repair (d) rebuild (e) copy
16. *Germane* most nearly means (a) fertile (b) pertinent (c) possible (d) sufficient (e) desirable
17. *Subterfuge* most nearly means (a) deception (b) alliance (c) scandal (d) plan (e) escape
18. *Dire* most nearly means (a) enough (b) pleasant (c) formidable (d) significant (e) extreme
19. *Diminutive* most nearly means (a) positive (b) intelligent (c) small (d) direct (e) helpful
20. *Arcane* most nearly means (a) distant (b) usual (c) conceited (d) mysterious (e) comprehensive

Test 3

From the choices given, select the word that most nearly means the same as the italicized word.

1. *Sanguine* (a) thorough (b) special (c) optimistic (d) particular (e) bright
2. *Precarious* (a) dangerous (b) stable (c) preventable (d) helpful (e) satisfying
3. *Intermittent* (a) frequent (b) regular (c) unusual (d) creative (e) periodic
4. *Appease* (a) create (b) decorate (c) calm (d) distribute (e) repeat
5. *Maelstrom* (a) congregation (b) turmoil (c) thunder (d) miracle (e) steadiness
6. *Mercurial* (a) changeable (b) balanced (c) inquiring (d) new (e) daily

7. *Dissipate* (a) disperse (b) brusque (c) happy (d) organized (e) beautiful

8. *Curt* (a) talented (b) brusque (c) happy (d) organized (e) courteous

9. *Interdict* (a) please (b) intertwine (c) remove (d) frequent (e) prohibit

10. *Indigent* (a) poor (b) indecent (c) dependent (d) unhappy (e) composed

11. *Altercation* (a) movement (b) perfection (c) beginning (d) quarrel (e) reparation

12. *Proffer* (a) offer (b) exit (c) return (d) proceed (e) spread

13. *Transient* (a) perpetual (b) changeable (c) short-lived (d) different (e) automatic

14. *Incessant* (a) irritating (b) secret (c) scarce (d) doubtful (e) unceasing

15. *Dogmatic* (a) animal-like (b) dictatorial (c) automatic (d) religious (e) efficient

16. *Obtuse* (a) dull (b) characteristic (c) fortunate (d) trustworthy (e) enthusiastic

17. *Stoic* (a) experienced (b) excited (c) average (d) impassive (e) perfect

18. *Vivid* (a) muddled (b) comparative (c) graphic (d) ancient (e) intelligent

19. *Voluble* (a) expectant (b) glib (c) domestic (d) enlightened (e) unstable

20. *Prosaic* (a) unimaginative (b) tragic (c) devoted (d) possible (e) ineffective

Test 4

Here you are concerned with *antonyms*. Choose the lettered word that is most nearly opposite in meaning to the italicized word.

1. *Punctual* (a) precise (b) dilatory (c) rare (d) concise (e) succinct
2. *Subsequent* (a) eventual (b) comparative (c) prior (d) subservient (e) succeeding
3. *Apropos* (a) pertinent (b) contrite (c) sensible (d) ancient (e) irrelevant
4. *Infringe* (a) respect (b) perceive (c) bestow (d) encircle (e) violate
5. *Succor* (a) neglect (b) arrange (c) administer (d) fragment (e) help
6. *Transitory* (a) temporary (b) bearable (c) permanent (d) troublesome (e) numerous
7. *Culpable* (a) responsible (b) obedient (c) innocent (d) immoral (e) anticipated
8. *Dogmatic* (a) reasonable (b) militant (c) expectant (d) rigorous (e) constrained
9. *Intrinsic* (a) necessary (b) basic (c) extraneous (d) magnificent (e) furtive
10. *Clandestine* (a) overt (b) secret (c) shadowy (d) brilliant (e) mellow
11. *Abridge* (a) offset (b) build (c) condense (d) discard (e) expand
12. *Restive* (a) simple (b) comfortable (c) reticent (d) hardy (e) patient
13. *Voluble* (a) large (b) fluent (c) reticent (d) complete (e) vexing
14. *Lachrymose* (a) happy (b) tearful (c) laden (d) brown (e) latent
15. *Migratory* (a) moveable (b) subversive (c) subtle (d) satisfied (e) stationary
16. *Orthodox* (a) sound (b) plentiful (c) usual (d) heretical (e) reactionary
17. *Prodigious* (a) abundant (b) minute (c) slow (d) deadly (e) amateurish

18. *Ingenuous* (a) real (b) rustic (c) everlasting (d) clever (e) flexible
19. *Capricious* (a) entertaining (b) steady (c) erratic (d) splendid (e) jovial
20. *Obfuscate* (a) aver (b) estrange (c) clarify (d) confuse (e) assemble

Test 5

Select the lettered pairs of words related to each other in the same way as the original words are related to each other.

1. *Transparent: Translucent*   (a) clear: foggy (b) night: day (c) black: white (d) frog: water (e) intelligent: dull

2. *Contemplation: Monk*   (a) quiet: noise (b) desk: chair (c) model: beauty (d) activity: salesman (e) reader: magazine

3. *Munificent: Philanthropist*   (a) inventive: scientist (b) searching: astronomer (c) competent: doctor (d) parsimonious: miser (e) circumspect: race car driver

4. *Abhor: Love*   (a) hope: despair (b) happiness: sorrow (c) like: enjoy (d) hate: disgust (e) fear: terror

5. *Elegy: Poetry*   (a) sing: bird (b) wheat: harvest (c) bread: flour (d) corn: grain (e) tractor: farm

6. *Nocturnal: Diurnal*   (a) annual: perennial (b) dark: light (c) pope: church (d) outside: inside (e) midnight: moon

7. *Obese: Emaciated*   (a) thin: slender (b) cavity: tooth (c) obsolete: new (d) lead: silver (e) twenty dollars: fifty dollars

8. *Gold: Ore*   (a) dear: cheap (b) iron: steel (c) pearls: oysters (d) steel: iron (e) intelligence: astuteness

9. *Carefulness: Safety*   (a) tires: automobile (b) siren: police car (c) frugality: security (d) binding: book (e) planning: success

10. *Aviary: Peacock*   (a) kennel: dog (b) fish: aquarium (c) warren: rabbit (d) covey: quail (e) cage: parrot

Test 6

Select in each series the word or word group that is closest in meaning to the word italicized in the phrase (sentence).

1. *Propriety* of actions (property/properness/standard/principle/behavior)
2. I replied *glibly*. (fast/profound/slowly/loudly/fluently)
3. Your reasoning is *erroneous*. (incorrect/convincing/right/pleasing/learned)

4. *Edified* by the sermon (pleased/disgusted/saddened/amused/ uplifted)
5. These fruits are *indigenous*. (common/expensive/sweet/ native/nonexistent)
6. *Harassed* by upperclassmen (praised/ignored/loved/ guided/tormented)
7. Completely *exasperated* (thoughtful/exalted/pleased/worn out/angered)
8. A *sagacious* decision (shrewd/foolish/unanimous/necessary/overdue)
9. To eat *voraciously* (rapidly/slowly/politely/indifferently/ greedily)
10. With much *vehemence* (pettiness/violence/venom/ expression/ease)
11. Religious *intolerance* (unwillingness/uneasiness/narrow-mindedness/faith/sincerity)
12. *Ostensibly* confused (much/unexpectedly/professedly/ possibly/stupidly)
13. An *antiquated* building (rustic/outdated/magnificent/ modern/haunted)
14. To *dominate* a converstion (improve/interrupt/participate in/rule/object to)
15. A *boon* to mankind (legacy/blessing/boost/friend/curse)
16. A *lucrative* occupation (dull/interesting/overcrowded/ lucky/profitable)
17. We *subjugated* the natives. (educated/clothed/conquered/harassed/victimized)
18. The action was *deplorable*. (useless/desirable/regrettable/necessary/decisive)
19. The child wept *copiously*. (little/abundantly/often/ secretly/openly)
20. Complete *annihilation* (destruction/praise/anger/despair/ victory)

21. A *peculiarity* of manners (politeness/quality/genuineness/change/oddity)
22. Acting *flippantly* (pertly/half-scared/half-apologetically/flinchingly/stupidly)
23. A *beatific* smile (silly/flashing/beaming/blissful/sincere)
24. To *succumb* to a disease (overcome/yield to/ignore/be immune to/be cured of)
25. A *colossal* undertaking (approved/amazing/huge/impossible/secret)

Test 7

Select the lettered word that is closest in meaning to the italicized word in the preceding phrase (sentence).

1. He *abetted* the conspirators.　(a) summoned (b) foiled (c) aided (d) imprisoned (e) beheaded

2. The clerk *absconded*.　(a) disagreed (b) forgot (c) disappeared (d) swore (e) resigned

3. A sharp *acclivity*　(a) slope (b) practice (c) criticism (d) pain (e) response

4. Spoken with *acerbity*　(a) authority (b) bitterness (c) ease (d) hesitancy (e) pride

5. An old *adage*　(a) house (b) utensil (c) saying (d) chamber (e) dance

6. *Adroitly* argued　(a) calmly (b) awkwardly (c) cleverly (d) hotly (e) frequently

7. The *altercation* was settled. (a) transaction (b) problem (c) territory (d) dispute (e) bill

8. An *antipathy* to war (a) preparation (b) demand (c) aversion (d) cause (e) enthusiasm

9. A *babel* of languages (a) similarity (b) decay (c) study (d) confusion (e) ignorance

10. His *baleful* influence (a) inspiring (b) helpful (c) constant (d) evil (e) welcome

11. With *benign* thoughts (a) sly (b) lofty (c) hypocritical (d) kindly (e) bitter

12. The teacher *berated* them. (a) graded (b) tested (c) scolded (d) dismissed (e) lauded

13. His *blatant* stupidity (a) loud-mouthed (b) childish (c) obvious (d) inherent (e) pathetic

14. A *bucolic* scene (a) touching (b) lively (c) warlike (d) rustic (e) deplorable

15. They *cached* their supplies. (a) consumed (b) stored (c) purchased (d) lost (e) discarded

16. He was a *charlatan*. (a) actor (b) impostor (c) spy (d) halfbreed (e) officer

17. With great *chagrin* (a) vexation (b) fuss (c) amusement (d) courage (e) ignorance

18. A *circuitous* route

    (a) forbidden (b) hazardous (c) short (d) roundabout (e) unused

19. They use *coercion*.

    (a) hypnotism (b) cooperation (c) care (d) force (e) discretion

20. *Commiserate* with me.

    (a) dine (b) sympathize (c) share (d) celebrate (e) compete

Test 8

For each numbered word select the best lettered definition on the right.

1. Amphibious
2. Agrarian
3. Autonomous
4. Empirical

    (a) based on observation or experiment
    (b) having two possible meanings
    (c) capable of working on both land and water
    (d) self-governing, independent
    (e) having to do with farming

5. Allocate
6. Reimburse
7. Facilitate
8. Curtail

    (a) make easier
    (b) reduce, diminish
    (c) take revenge on
    (d) make payment for expense or loss
    (e) set apart for a special purpose

9. Depreciation
10. Collateral
11. Dilemma
12. Assets

    (a) situation requiring a hard choice
    (b) property or cash possessed
    (c) an unfavorable characterization
    (d) decrease in value through use
    (e) security pledged for repayment of a loan

13.	Liaison	(a)	vital statistics
14.	Reciprocity	(b)	gradual payment of a debt before the due date
15.	Arbitration	(c)	bond or connection between persons or groups
16.	Amortization	(d)	settling a dispute with the help of a referee
		(e)	mutual exchange

17.	Strategy	(a)	an addition to a will
18.	Reparations	(b)	reduction of a bill for prompt payment
19.	Codicil	(c)	set of laws
20.	Discount	(d)	skillful management in a contest
		(e)	payment for damage inflicted

Test 9

Match each numbered word with its lettered definition.

1.	Reciprocity	(a)	to set apart for a special purpose
2.	Amphibious	(b)	to make payment for expense or loss
3.	Arbitration	(c)	skillful management to get the better of an opponent
4.	Allocate	(d)	decrease in value through use
5.	Amortization	(e)	property or cash possessed
6.	Reimburse	(f)	mutual exchange
7.	Strategy	(g)	having to do with farm matters
8.	Agrarian	(h)	capable of working on both land and water
9.	Reparations	(i)	an addition to a will
10.	Depreciation	(j)	security pledged for payment of a loan
11.	Codicil	(k)	make easier

12.	Collateral	(l)	become worse
13.	Facilitate	(m)	compensation by a defeated nation for damage after a war
14.	Dilemma	(n)	self-governing, independent
15.	Autonomous	(o)	amount subtracted from a bill for prompt payment or other special reason
16.	Assets	(p)	gradual payment of a debt before the due date
17.	Curtail	(q)	to reduce, diminish
18.	Deteriorate	(r)	a difficult or embarrassing situation
19.	Discount	(s)	bond or connection between persons or groups
20.	Liaison	(t)	settling a dispute by discussing and coming to an agreement

Test 10

Select the lettered word or word group that is closest in meaning to the italicized word in the preceding phrase (sentence).

1. An *aura* of culture
   (a) age (b) air (c) absence (d) source (e) history

2. That *banal* joke
   (a) funny (b) foul (c) mean (d) coy (e) trite

3. She looked *comatose*.
   (a) innocent (b) purple (c) unconscious (d) comical (e) repulsive

4. *Construe* this paragraph.
   (a) translate (b) omit (c) rewrite (d) copy (e) memorize

5. An attractive *décor* (a) decoration (b) voice (c) gathering (d) title (e) clergyman

6. An *epitome* of the novel (a) duplicate (b) continuation (c) summary (d) revision (e) climax

7. Don't *equivocate!* (a) be offensive (b) be cowardly (c) be skeptical (d) be ambiguous (e) be optimistic

8. The plot was a *fiasco*. (a) mutiny (b) failure (c) secret (d) massacre (e) hoax

9. A *gregarious* people (a) vegetarian (b) agricultural (c) barbaric (d) sociable (e) enviable

10. *Histrionic* speeches (a) theatrical (b) hysterical (c) impolite (d) historic (e) repetitious

11. He *instigated* the revolt. (a) ignored (b) blamed (c) spurred on (d) reported (e) repressed

12. Their annual *kermis* (a) pilgrimage (b) reunion (c) tax (d) festival (e) epidemic

13. His *myrmidons* departed. (a) chariots (b) entertainers (c) henchmen (d) mourners (e) vessels

14. An *opalescent* dawn (a) belated (b) opal-tinted (c) cold gray (d) storm-shrouded (e) tropical

15. She *parried* his question. (a) pondered (b) mocked (c) echoed (d) evaded (e) resented

16. Her *penurious* aunt
   (a) inquisitive (b) stingy (c) penniless (d) supposed (e) peevish

17. Let us *remonstrate*.
   (a) return (b) confer (c) retire (d) protest (e) disband

18. *Stringent* laws
   (a) unjust (b) ridiculous (c) severe (d) obsolete (e) obscure

19. A *tyro* in dramatics
   (a) villain (b) crisis (c) beginner (d) problem (e) failure

20. He behaved like a *zany*.
   (a) gypsy (b) baby (c) maniac (d) tyrant (e) clown

Test 11

Match each numbered word with its lettered definition.

1.	Ambidextrous	(a)	a hater of mankind
2.	Assiduous	(b)	haughtily disdainful
3.	Cacophony	(c)	cowardly
4.	Elucidate	(d)	disgrace or reproach incurred by conduct considered shameful
5.	Grandiose	(e)	formal expression of praise
6.	Innocuous	(f)	logically unsound
7.	Invective	(g)	able to use both hands equally well
8.	Misanthrope	(h)	constant in application
9.	Ostentatious	(i)	false argument
10.	Supercilious	(j)	not harmful
11.	Vicarious	(k)	affectedly grand
12.	Encomium	(l)	make clear
13.	Concatenation	(m)	experienced in place of another
14.	Abscond	(n)	having one's identity concealed

15.	Fallacious	(o)	harsh sound
16.	Nebulous	(p)	to run away to avoid legal process
17.	Pusillanimous	(q)	vague, hazy, cloudy
18.	Sophistry	(r)	an utterance of violent reproach or accusation
19.	Incognito	(s)	state of being linked together
20.	Opprobrium	(t)	characterized by show

Test 12

The word *allow* has several synonyms, among them *let, permit, suffer,* and *tolerate*. Are there other synonyms for *let?*

Test 13

The word *choice* has several synonyms. Name at least five.

Test 14

Give one antonym for each of the following: *arrive, atrocious, arrogant, dark, latent, solitary, sophisticated, temporary, weak, wordy*.

Test 15

Find the group of words on the right that fits the numbered word on the left. Then select the word in the numbered and lettered group on the right with the shade of meaning given in parentheses.

1. Bad
   (1a) guard (1b) protect (1c) support (1d) shield (1e) preserve (put a barrier against immediate harm)

2. Heavy   (2a) structure (2b) edifice (2c) pile (2d) tower (2e) monument (archaic or poetic)

3. Play   (3a) ill (3b) sinister (3c) evil (3d) wicked (3e) naughty (presaging something)

4. Murmur   (4a) force (4b) power (4c) energy (4d) might (4e) puissance (most poetic)

5. Greedy   (5a) fault (5b) failing (5c) foible (5d) vice (5e) weakness (most unfavorable connotation)

6. Enthusiasm   (6a) weighty (6b) hefty (6c) massive (6d) ponderous (6e) cumbersome (labored or dull)

7. Faithful   (7a) sport (7b) frolic (7c) romp (7d) gamble (7e) oscillate (lighthearted, carefree)

8. Strength   (8a) loyal (8b) constant (8c) staunch (8d) resolute (8e) trustworthy (freedom from fickleness)

9. Defend   (9a) passion (9b) spirit (9c) ardor (9d) fervor (9e) zeal (for an object or cause)

10. Building   (10a) mutter (10b) mumble (10c) whisper (10d) grumble (10e) gurgle (in an angry or surly way)

      (11a) avaricious (11b) avid (11c) grasping (11d) covetous (11e) esurient (from the Latin ''to eat'')

Test 16

Find the group of words on the right that is *opposite* in meaning to the numbered word on the left. Then select the word in the lettered group with the shade of meaning given in parentheses.

1. Fair   (1a) orderly (1b) systematic (1c) controlled (planned)

2. Lean   (2a) rapid (2b) quick (2c) fast (also means "alive")

3. Obscure   (3a) sane (3b) sound (3c) healthy (applies also to inanimate things)

4. Free   (4a) fat (4b) obese (4c) plump (least unfavorable connotation)

5. Pleasant   (5a) tiny (5b) minute (5c) small (hard to see)

6. Slow   (6a) biased (6b) partial (6c) prejudiced (slanted)

7. Huge   (7a) crude (7b) rough (7c) raw (unprocessed)

8. Fabulous   (8a) clear (8b) distinct (8c) obvious (plain, evident)

9. Chaotic   (9a) credible (9b) plausible (9c) literal (may be deceptive)

10. Refined   (10a) inhibited (10b) contained (10c) bound (held back, withheld)

(11a) upsetting (11b) distasteful (11c) distressing (repellent)

17

Fun with Words

1. The shortest words in English are "a," "I," and "O." What's the longest?

2. Use your imagination and your dictionary to answer these odd questions:

1. What are a squeegee, a trochee, a manatee, a banshee, the Pee Dee?
2. What is the meaning of each of these puzzle favorites: stoa, proa, moa, goa, boa?
3. Can *cabbage* be used as a verb?
4. What might you get if you ordered escargots, à la king, escarole, roast beef au jus, à la Newburg?
5. Can *how* be a noun?

3. An *anagram* is the reordering of the letters of a word or phrase to form another word or phrase: pots, post, stop, tops. Rearrange the letters of the following words or group of words to form the word or name defined or indicated.

1. dread—a viper
2. atom—a ditch
3. act divine—to clear from suspicion
4. tory—a beginner
5. coiled—submissive
6. attic—unspoken
7. tome—a speck of dust
8. glide—cold
9. wary—twisted
10. We all make his praise—writer

. The "venereal game" has nothing to do with love, disease, or sex. Its meaning comes from a Latin word meaning "to hunt game or animals." Thus *venery* is an archaic word referring to hunting, a chase that has given rise to some unusual names for groups of hunted objects, domestic animals, and birds. What are the names for collections of ants, toads, martens, ponies, lapwings, larks, finches, mules, hawks, bears, nightingales, rabbits, whales, sheep, swine?

. There are additional remarkable names for collections of fish, birds, and other animals. We speak of a "gaggle" of geese and a "pride" of lions. How would you refer to a collection or group of elephants, pups, bees, hens, foxes, leopards, rooks, kittens, angels, starlings, fish, pheasants, elk, locusts?

. Pair a word from column 1 with one from column 2, moving in either direction, to form a six-letter word.

but	her	bed	for
car	ace	set	cup
rot	bar	age	war
per	lam	wit	son
wit	ten	tea	pet
den	sun	let	sup
men	dim	par	ham
ley	ton		

7. Place a letter before each of these words to form a word that has the asked-for meaning.

1. ache—hide away
2. align—slander
3. trophy—wither away
4. toll—coral island
5. rate—angry
6. hasten—punish

7. raven—coward
8. love—a spice
9. lithe—joyous
10. edition—treason
11. bet—encourage
12. aster—small wheel

8. *Sexism* may be broadly defined as "discrimination against women." Some advocates of liberation would change "spokesman" to "spokesperson" and "chairman" to "chairperson" or simply "chair." "Postman" can easily be changed to "postperson" and "middleman" to "middleperson." Just for fun—and not to get into any arguments—what can you do with *fisher marks, ikin, hole, super, woods, hour, hunt, work, made, hench power, sword, trap?*

9. Some words include unlikely combinations of letters such as XYG (oxygen), HEON (luncheon), and TOMO (automobile). What words contain the following combinations?

1. PHYT
2. ZOPH
3. RIJU
4. SYNTH
5. RND

6. DHP
7. XOPH
8. MIKA
9. ERGRO

10. With numerous words the first part is a verb, the second part is that verb's direct object: *breakfast, cutthroat.* List a number of other verb-noun words.

11. Some words spelled backward form another word as, for example, *deliver* can become *reviled*. List some other turnabouts such as *pan* and *part*.

12. Search your memory and your dictionary for words that contain five or more consecutive consonants such as *crypt* and *psychosis*. What others can you list?

13. An *acronym* is a word formed from the initial letters of a name (WAC for Women's Army Corps) or by combining initial letters as parts of a series of words (LORAN from "long range navigation"). As you list other acronyms be sure to study how they are formed (RADAR—radio detecting and ranging).

14. A *palindrome* is a word, phrase, or sentence that reads the same forward or backward; *radar, level, refer*. List as many palindromes as you can.

15. A *reversible* word is one capable of being turned around (reversed). For example, "overhang" can be reversed to read "hang over"; "overrun" can become "run over." Think of other reversible words.

16. What might you get in your favorite eating place if you ordered as follows?

  1. A ruddy sphere pie and a polygonal curd of milk separated from whey.
  2. A cylinder between two halves of another cylindrical object.
  3. A cylinder of curd and a patty on an oblate spheroid.

17. Lewis Carroll, the famous author, invented a game he called "Doublets." It is played by altering one word into another through changing one letter at a time, each step resulting in a new, valid word. He changed *four* into *five* this way: four, foul, fool, foot, fort, fore, fire, five. Change each of the following, all of them Carroll's examples.

chin into *nose*   *poor* into *rich*
tears into *smile*   *winter* into *summer*

18. A physician is a doctor of medicine, but many doctors have specialties. Can you place the following?

1. internist
2. cardiologist
3. neurologist
4. syphilologist
5. orthopedist

6. dermatologist
7. pediatrician
8. gynecologist
9. urologist
10. obstetrician

19. Words have interesting life stories just as people do. With the help of your dictionary or other reference books, find out how, when, and where the following words came into being.

1. Titan
2. mecca
3. pariah
4. nemesis
5. Thespian

6. crisscross
7. admiral
8. shanghai
9. meander
10. hegira

20. The name of a city or American state is hidden in each of the following sentences. In each sentence, letters forming the name appear in consecutive order.

1. August always has several hot days.
2. My father enjoys his den very much.
3. The poet Goethe wrote his epic poem *Faust* in 1805.

4. We got rent on the first of each month.
5. Can Eva dance well?
6. You will soon find that gumbo is easy to make.
7. My main evil was greed.
8. Lewis cons Indians every day.
9. Papa rises early on feast days.
10. You might exasperate your mother.
11. Nine vehicles were parked outside.
12. Aren't you afraid a hobo will bother you?

21. Latin is called a dead language, but it lives in many common words. Can you define these examples?

1.	regimen	6.	terminus
2.	mores	7.	interim
3.	tedium	8.	opus
4.	latitude	9.	radius
5.	placebo	10.	status

22. How's your knowledge of colors? Match the color named in the left-hand column with its description in the right-hand column.

1.	maroon	(a)	sky blue
2.	pink	(b)	cherry red
3.	mauve	(c)	bright bluish-red
4.	azure	(d)	vivid blue
5.	fuchsia	(e)	deep purplish-red
6.	crimson	(f)	purplish rose
7.	vermilion	(g)	dark brownish-red
8.	cerise	(h)	dark yellow
9.	cerulean	(i)	brilliant scarlet-red
10.	ocher	(j)	light crimson

23. When you next visit a doctor's office and get tired of looking at old magazines, while away the time by trying to define these medical terms:

1.	platelet	6.	trauma
2.	hypochondriac	7.	obese
3.	vascular	8.	intravenous
4.	atrophy	9.	psychosomatic
5.	toxic	10.	comatose

24. You know that a *hypnotist* can induce a sleeplike condition in which an individual is responsive to suggestions. But do you know who or what are the areas of concern of the following "ists"?

1.	anthropologist	6.	entomologist
2.	geologist	7.	oenologist
3.	botanist	8.	sociologist
4.	zoologist	9.	oculist
5.	philologist	10.	otolaryngologist

25. Would you like to know the specialties of still other trained men and women? What do the following persons do?

1.	anesthetist	6.	orthodontist
2.	etymologist	7.	ichthyologist
3.	ophthalmologist	8.	podiatrist
4.	chiropodist	9.	ecologist
5.	lexicographer	10.	agronomist

26. A *Briticism* is a word, phrase, or expression characteristic of British English as compared to American English. For example, if you were living in England, you might stop to buy *petrol* for your car, not *gasoline*. Translate the following Briticisms into American English.

1.	lorry	6.	flat	11.	biscuit	16.	circus	
2.	sweets	7.	spanner	12.	accumulator	17.	dustbin	
3.	bonnet	8.	loo	13.	metalled road	18.	chemist	
4.	lift	9.	treacle	14.	boot	19.	braces	
5.	pram	10.	chips	15.	wing	20.	bird (slang)	

27. An *eponym* is a person for whom something is named or a person so prominently connected with something as to be a designation for it. "Romulus" is the eponym of *Rome*. An eponym is also a real or mythical person whose name is, or is thought to be, the source of the name of a city, country, era, or institution. Our language keeps alive the names of hundreds of persons and places. Each of the following articles or materials of wearing apparel is named for an individual or group. Your dictionary will help if you are stumped.

1. loose trousers worn under a skirt
2. a sock knitted in diamond shapes
3. a sweater opening down the front
4. a soft felt hat
5. a heavy, strong twilled cotton
6. a snugly fitting elastic garment
7. a rubberized raincoat
8. a loose coat, jacket, or sweater
9. a coarse twilled cloth
10. a kind of overcoat

28. Here are still more eponyms. Can you trace their origins?

1.	atlas	4.	melba	7.	Fahrenheit	10.	saxophone
2.	macadam	5.	sandwich	8.	poinsettia	11.	iris
3.	cereal	6.	ampere	9.	davenport	12.	galvanize

| 13. | volt | 16. | odyssey | 17. | valentine | 19. | calico |
| 14. | magnolia | 15. | braille | 18. | tantalize | 20. | shrapnel |

29. What kind of person are you? What types of people do you like? Find out. Match the types of men and women in the left-hand column with their descriptions in the right-hand column.

1.	hoyden	(a)	a sharp-tongued scold
2.	Don Juan	(b)	a powerful businessman
3.	coquette	(c)	a handsome man
4.	shrew	(d)	coy
5.	minx	(e)	a tomboy
6.	cavalier	(f)	a flirt
7.	virago	(g)	a gallant
8.	tycoon	(h)	a saucy girl
9.	Adonis	(i)	a nag
10.	demure	(j)	a rake

30. In the number and variety of its borrowed words English is unique among languages. Over many centuries English has become the most democratic and cosmopolitan of all languages. Each word in the following list has come from another language, country, or city. Indicate the origin of each word.

1.	flannel	6.	oasis	11.	garage	16.	ukulele
2.	alcohol	7.	alias	12.	apartheid	17.	ersatz
3.	banshee	8.	presto	13.	corral	18.	vodka
4.	tattoo	9.	jackal	14.	canoe	19.	boss
5.	bayou	10.	kibitzer	15.	boomerang	20.	bazaar

110

ANSWERS TO
Quizzes

1. No objective answer is possible.

2. 1. c; 2. b; 3. d; 4. a; 5. d

3. 1. e; 2. d; 3. c; 4. b; 5. c

4. 1. d; 2. d; 3. b; 4. c; 5. d

5. Answers will vary slightly depending upon the dictionary being used, but here is applicable information:
   1. From *tele* (a combining form meaning ''far off,'' ''at a distance'') and *scope* (range of view, from Italian *scope*, Latin *scopus*, Greek *skopos*).
   2. From Middle French *panique*, from Greek *panikos* (of or for the god Pan, who was believed to cause sudden or groundless fear).
   3. From Medieval Latin *manufactura* (*manus*, hand + *factura*, a making; *factus*, the past participle of *facere*, to make).
   4. From Latin *professus*, the past participle of *profiteri*,

to avow, to confess (*pro,* before + *fateri,* to confess).

5. From the French, after Jean Nicot (1530–1600), French courtier who introduced tobacco into France from Portugal.

6. From Latin *April (is),* virtually unchanged as the word has come through Old English, Old French, and Middle English.

6. attack, attacked
dived, dove; dived, dove
wrung, wrung
drew, drawn
bit, bitten
leaped, leapt; leaped, leapt
swore, sworn
awoke, awaked; awoke, awakened
smelled, smelt; smelled, smelt
set, set

made, made
sent, sent
won, won
spelled, spelt; spelled, spelt
took, taken
paid, paid
fought, fought
brought, brought
came, come
grew, grown

7.
1. analyses
2. antennae
3. mongooses
4. moose
5. leaves
6. strata, stratums
7. halves
8. phenomena, phenomenons
9. hypotheses
10. criteria, criterions
11. summonses
12. alumni (alumnae)
13. crises
14. spoonfuls
15. stimuli

8. No final answer is possible.

9. Answers will vary depending upon the dictionary consulted. Here is a consensus listing:

112

1. informal for *bologna,* slang   4. informal
   for *nonsense*   5. informal
2. no label   6. Scotland and
3. dialectal   northern England

10.
1. agent, ambiguous, counteract, agenda, agile, actor
2. audience, auditorium, inaudible, audition, auditor
3. automobile, autograph, autonomous, autocrat, automatic
4. exclaim, declaim, clamor, proclamation, exclamation
5. cordial, record, accord, concord, discord, concordance
6. succumb, incumbent, incubator, cubicle, recumbent
7. produce, abduct, conduct, introduction, reduce
8. equation, equivocate, adequate, equilibrium, equivalent
9. confirm, affirm, infirmary, infirm, confirmation
10. bigamy, polygamy, monogamous, exogamy, monogamy

11.
1. geology, geometry, apogee, geography, geophysics
2. gratuity, congratulate, gratitude, grateful, gratify
3. conjunction, conjugal, junction, adjoin, juncture
4. select, eligible, election, collect, elect, selection
5. monitor, admonish, monument, premonition, monumental
6. move, motive, automobile, emotion, promote, remote
7. native, nature, nascent, nation, natal, prenatal
8. propel, expulsion, repulsive, compel, impel, repel
9. petition, appetite, compete, competitor, competent
10. deposit, composite, component, compose, postpone

12.
1. preside, sedentary, session, reside, sediment, sedate
2. spectator, inspector, perspicacity, conspicuous, spectacle
3. intact, tangible, contact, tangent, tactile
4. revert, versatile, avert, convert, conversation, divert
5. invisible, television, provide, evident, vision, visitor
6. revolve, revolution, volume, involve, revolt, evolve
7. century, centigrade, centipede, centenary, centenarian
8. doctrine, docile, doctor, document, documentary
9. deflect, reflection, circumflex, flexible, inflection
10. cohere, coherence, adhere, adhesive, inherent, incoherent

13.
1. cern- (cret-)
2. ger- (gest-)
3. ab- (abs-)
4. pre-
5. intra-
6. post-
7. bio-
8. flu- (flux)
9. pat-, (pass-)
10. cal-

14.
1. *aristos*—the best: *Aristocracy* consists of persons holding exceptional rank or privilege.
2. *beatus*—blessed: Relief from extreme pain is *beatific*.
3. *causa*—cause, reason: What was the *causal* force that made you do this?
4. *decem*—ten: In ancient Rome, *December* was the tenth month of the year.
5. *hostis*—enemy: The atmosphere in the courtroom was *hostile*.
6. *mater*—mother: Rosa had a *maternal* attitude toward the puppy.
7. *pedi*—foot: A *pedometer* is an instrument for record-

ing the number of steps taken in walking, thus show-
ing the number of feet or miles traveled.

8. *petra*—rock: *Petroleum* is sometimes referred to as
   "rock oil."

9. *plus*—many: Our candidate won by a large *plurality*.

10. *umbra*—offense, resentment: The policeman took
    umbrage at my comments.

15.

1. B	7. C	13. D	19. A
2. E	8. B	14. C	20. E
3. D	9. B	15. B	21. B
4. A	10. A	16. A	22. D
5. A	11. E	17. D	23. E
6. D	12. D	18. C	24. C

16.

25. B	31. C	37. C	43. A
26. C	32. B	38. A	44. C
27. A	33. C	39. B	45. C
28. D	34. A	40. D	46. E
29. E	35. B	41. B	47. A
30. D	36. D	42. E	48. D

17. two —Greek *di* as in *dichloride, dicho* as in *dichotomy;*
       Latin *bi* as in *bicycle* and *bigamy*.

   six —Greek *hexa* as in *hexagonal;* Latin *sex* as in *sex-
       tet.*

   seven—Greek *hepta* as in *heptameter;* Latin *sept* as in
       September.

   eight —Greek *oct* as in *octagonal;* Latin *oct* as in *October*
       and *octave*.

   nine —Greek *ennea* as in *ennead;* Latin *nov* or *non* as in
       November and *nonagon*.

ten —Greek *deca* as in *decade;* Latin *dec (deci)* as in *December* and *decimal.*

half —Greek *hemi* as in *hemisphere;* Latin *semi* as in *semicircle* and *demi* as in *demitasse.*

18. *bi-*: two, twice, doubly—biannual, bicameral, bicentennial, bicycle, bilingual

cross-: going across, counter—crossroad, crossbar, cross-eyed, cross-breed, cross-examine

non-: not—nonabsorbent, nonaggression, nonbreakable, nondescript, nonplus

pre-: prior to, in advance, early—preschool, prewar, preference, prehistoric, prepaid

sub-: under, below, secretly—subway, subtract, subversion, substation, sublet

19. 1. amoral, anonymous
    2. ambiguous, ambidextrous
    3. audition, audiovisual
    4. biology, biography
    5. collection, collateral
    6. enact, empower
    7. epilogue, epigram
    8. hemisphere, hemicycle
    9. illogical, illegitimate
    10. neophyte, neolithic
    11. parachute, paragraph
    12. perimeter, perigee
    13. pseudonym, pseudoclassic
    14. ultrasonic, ultraviolet
    15. unfair, unbend

20. 1. under, beneath (hypodermic)
    2. within (intramurals)

3. with, together (synchronize)
4. different (heterogeneous)
5. same (homogenous)
6. correct, straight (orthodontist)
7. all (omniscient)
8. power (dynamo)
9. king, queen (regal)
10. city (urban)
11. world, universe (cosmonaut)
12. love (philanthropist)
13. fear, aversion (acrophobia)
14. faith (fidelity)
15. belief (credible)
16. lead (induct)
17. turmoil (disturbance)
18. break (interrupt)
19. good, well (benefit)
20. wrong, evil (malice)

21. Because full answers would run for many pages, you are on your own. But start at the beginning: *primary, secondary,* etc.

22. -*al*:   of, related to, characterized by—optional, directional, fictional, withdrawal, national

-*est*:   suffix of the superlative—latest, highest, longest, hardest, luckiest

-*less*:   destitute of, without—childless, luckless, witless, peerless, countless

-*ist*:   characteristic of, relating to, one who does—bicyclist, apologist, dramatist, machinist, internist

-*ment*:   concrete result, means, or instrument—refreshment, embankment, entertainment, amazement, ornament

23.
1. Americana, collegiana
2. connivance, nonchalance
3. freedom, kingdom
4. twofold, manifold
5. harmful, beautiful
6. novice, apprentice
7. plagiarism, barbarism
8. civility, nobility

24.
1. *mono-* (one)—monologue, monosyllable, monochrome, monogamy, monogram
2. *non-* (not)—noncombatant, noncommittal, nonconformist, nondistinctive, nonrestrictive
3. *pseudo-* (false)—pseudonym, pseudoclassic, pseudonymous, pseudomorph, pseudoscience
4. *semi-* (half)—semiannual, semiautomatic, semiautonomous, semicentennial, semicolon
5. *over-* (above, beyond)—overact, overlord, overextend, overhead, overpass
6. *micro-* (small)—microscopic, micrometer, microphone, microcosm, microwave
7. *auto-* (self)—automatic, autobiography, automobile, autocrat, autograph
8. *sub-* (below)—subway, suburb, subservient, submerge, submit
9. *bi-* (two)—biped, biannual, bifocals, bilinear, bilingual
10. *multi-* (many)—multitude, multiply, multiphase, multiracial, multilateral
11. *-est* (most)—easiest, fastest, fairest, tallest, hardest
12. *-able* (ability)—capable, knowledgeable, arable, receivable, repairable
13. *-ment* (act of, result of, means)—increment, retirement, equipment, instrument, ornament
14. *-graph* (write, impress)—photograph, autograph, telegraph, phonograph, pantograph
15. *-ish* (resembling)—childish, foolish, selfish, boyish, greenish

16. *-let* (small)—bracelet, ringlet, rivulet, epaulet, cutlet
17. *-ness* (state, condition, quality, degree)—goodness, baseness, easiness, laziness, awareness
18. *-like* (similar to)—godlike, childlike, statesmanlike, birdlike, lifelike
19. *-er* (one who does)—doer, worker, teacher, welder, driver
20. *-ine* (belonging to a group or class)—canine, feminine, masculine, feline, aquiline

25. *As a noun:* option, selection, preference, election, alternative
    As an adjective: exquisite, elegant, rare, delicate, dainty

26. *As a verb:* hire, assign, hire out, lease, rent
    As a noun: hindrance, impediment, obstacle, obstruction

27. 1. *street*—road, roadway, highway, highroad, avenue, boulevard, terrace, drive, parkway, thoroughfare, byway, lane, alley, alleyway
     2. *opposite*—contradictory, contrary, antithetical, antipodal, antonymous
     3. *frank*—candid, open, plain
     4. *answer* (verb)—respond, reply, rejoin, retort;
        (noun)—response, reply, rejoinder
     5. *trite*—hackneyed, stereotyped, threadbare, shopworn
     6. *defame*—vilify, calumniate, malign, traduce, asperse, slander, libel
     7. *yield*—submit, capitulate, succumb, relent, defer, bow, cave in
     8. *magic*—sorcery, witchcraft, witchery, wizardry, alchemy, thaumaturgy

9. *tolerant*—forbearing, lenient, indulgent, clement, merciful
10. *effort*—exertion, pains, trouble

28.
1. *professional*—amateur, dilettante, tyro
2. *solicitous*—unmindful, negligent
3. *huge*—small, little, diminutive, petite, wee, tiny, minute, microscopic, miniature
4. *repudiate*—adopt, acknowledge, own, admit, avow, embrace, espouse
5. *petty*—mammoth, enormous, immense, important, gross, momentous, huge
6. *decrease*—increase, augment, multiply, enlarge
7. *grave*—gay, light, frivolous, flighty
8. *sophisticated*—genuine, natural, naive, simple
9. *fine*—coarse, rough
10. *arrogant*—meek, unassuming, humble, lowly, submissive

ANSWERS TO
Test Yourself

Test 1

1. e 2. h 3. p 4. t 5. j 6. g 7. q 8. m 9. r 10. n
11. a 12. b 13. s 14. 1 15. k 16. i 17. f 18. d 19. c
20. o

Test 2

1. c 2. b 3. a 4. e 5. b 6. d 7. c 8. e 9. a 10. c
11. c 12. e 13. b 14. c 15. a 16. b 17. a 18. e
19. c 20. d

Test 3

1. c 2. a 3. e 4. c 5. b 6. a 7. a 8. b 9. e 10. a
11. d 12. a 13. c 14. e 15. b 16. a 17. d 18. c
19. b 20. a

Test 4

1. b 2. c 3. e 4. a 5. a 6. c 7. c 8. a 9. c 10. a
11. e 12. e 13. c 14. a 15. e 16. d 17. b 18. d
19. b 20. c

Test 5

1. a 2. d 3. d 4. a or b 5. d 6. b 7. c 8. d 9. e
10. a, c, or e

Test 6

1. properness
2. fluently
3. incorrect
4. uplifted
5. native
6. tormented
7. angered
8. shrewd
9. greedily
10. violence
11. narrowmindedness
12. professedly
13. outdated
14. rule
15. blessing
16. profitable
17. conquered
18. regrettable
19. abundantly
20. destruction
21. oddity
22. pertly
23. blissful
24. yield to
25. huge

Test 7

1. c 2. c 3. a 4. b 5. c 6. c 7. d 8. c 9. d 10. d
11. d 12. c 13. a 14. d 15. b 16. b 17. a 18. d
19. d 20. b

Test 8

1. c 2. e 3. d 4. a 5. e 6. d 7. a 8. b 9. d 10. e
11. a 12. b 13. c 14. e 15. d 16. b 17. d 18. e
19. a 20. b

Test 9

1. f 2. h 3. t 4. a 5. p 6. b 7. c 8. g 9. m 10. d
11. i 12. j 13. k 14. r 15. n 16. e 17. q 18. l 19. o
20. s

Test 10

1. b 2. e 3. c 4. a 5. a 6. c 7. d 8. b 9. d 10. a
11. c 12. d 13. c 14. b 15. d 16. b 17. d 18. c
19. c 20. e

Test 11

1. g 2. h 3. o 4. l 5. k 6. j 7. r 8. a 9. t 10. b
11. m 12. e 13. s 14. p 15. f 16. q 17. c 18. i
19. n 20. d

Test 12

As verb: hire, assign, hire out, lease, rent
As noun: hindrance, impediment, obstacle, obstruction

Test 13

As noun: option, selection, preference, election, alternative
As adj.: exquisite, elegant, rare, delicate, dainty

Test 14

arrive:	depart, leave, withdraw, retire
atrocious:	humane, virtuous, noble, genteel, righteous
arrogant:	meek, unassuming, modest, humble, submissive
dark:	light, bright, brilliant, radiant, luminous
latent:	patent, evident, manifest, obvious, apparent, palpable
solitary:	accompanied, attended, escorted, convoyed
sophisticated:	naive, simple, natural, artless, ingenuous
temporary:	permanent, lasting, stable, perpetual, perdurable
weak:	strong, stout, sturdy, tenacious, stalwart
wordy:	concise, terse, succinct, compressed, pithy

Test 15

1. 3b 2. 6d 3. 7b 4. 10d 5. 11e 6. 9e 7. 8b 8. 4e
9. 1d 10. 2c

Test 16

1. 6a 2. 4c 3. 8c 4. 10a 5. 11b 6. 2b 7. 5b 8. 9b
9. 1b 10. 7c

123

ANSWERS TO
Fun with Words

1. The usual answer is *antidisestablishmentarianism.* Used in 1869 by Prime Minister William Gladstone of Great Britain to describe the principles of those opposed to the separation of Church and State, this word contains twenty-eight letters. It exceeds by just one letter the word *honorificabilitudinitatibus,* which appears in the fifth act of Shakespeare's *Love's Labour's Lost.*

   Actually, these two novelty words are shorter than several others even less known. The word *floccinaucinihilipilification,* meaning "estimation as worthless," has twenty-nine letters; it was used in 1741 by Shenstone, in 1816 by Southey, and in 1829 by Scott. *Pneumonoultramicroscopicsilicovolcanokoniosis,* meaning "a disease of the lungs," contains forty-five letters. The word *aqueosalinocalcalinocetaceoaluminosocupreovitriolic,* however, used by an eighteenth-century doctor to describe the chemical qualities of the spa waters at Bristol, England, England, takes top place with fifty-one letters.

2. (1) An implement for removing water; a metrical foot; an aquatic animal; a supernatural being; a river in North and South Carolina.

(2) Portico; South Pacific boat; extinct bird; gazelle; snake or neckpiece.

(3) Yes, as a verb meaning "to steal," "to filch."

(4) Snails; diced meat or poultry in a cream sauce with mushrooms, green pepper, and pimento; beef in its own gravy; seafood cooked with a sauce of cream, egg yolks, and wine.

(5) Yes, when it means "method" or "manner."

3. adder, moat, vindicate, tyro, docile, tacit, mote, gelid, awry, William Shakespeare

4. colony, knot, richness, string, desert, exultation, charm, barren, cast, sleuth, watch, nest, gam, flock, saunder

5. herd, litter, swarm, brood, skulk, leap, clamor, kindle, host, murmuration, school, bouquet, gang, plague

6. button, carpet, rotten, supper, wither, warden, menace, barley, bedlam, sunset, forage, dimwit, teacup, hamlet, parson

7. cache, malign, atrophy, atoll, irate, chasten, craven, clove, blithe, sedition, abet, caster

8. fisherperson, marksperson, personikin, personhole, superperson, woodsperson, personhour, personhunt, workperson, personmade, henchperson, personpower, swordsperson, persontrap

9. neophyte, schizophrenia, marijuana, synthetic, dirndl, dry goods, jodhpur, saxophone, mikado, underground

10. killjoy, hangdog, carryall, turncoat, backspace, spoilsport, breakneck, scatterbrain, tripline, dive bomber, telltale, passport, scapegrace, scofflaw, wheelchair, checkpoint, catchpenny, breakfront

11. era, are; dessert, tressed; stinker, reknits; straw, warts; note, Eton; diaper, repaid; sore, Eros; deer, reed; live, evil; keep, peek; snap, pans; pit, tip; raw, war; tap, pat; laid, dial

12. synthetic, borscht, styptic, skyscraper, sylph, psychology, rhythm, symphonic, erstwhile, synchronize, earthshaking, birthplace, tryst, worthwhile, sphygmomanometer, strychnine

13. scuba, CORE, NATO, SEATO, zip, snafu, laser

14. nun, gig, Hannah, deified, bob, bib, dud, ewe, eye, kayak, rotator, noon, civic, tenet, redder, sexes, peep. These sentences form palindromes:
   Madam, I'm Adam.
   Was it a rat I saw?
   Able was I ere I saw Elba.
   In a regal age ran I.

15. outlay, layout; overwork, work over; outcome, come out; upend, end up; overall, all over; downfall, fall down; income, come in; overtake, take over; upsweep, sweep up; inland, land in

16. (1) apple pie and a wedge of cheese (2) a hot dog (frankfurter) on a bun (3) a cheeseburger

17. chin, coin, corn, core, cote, note, nose
    tears, sears, stars, stare, stale, stile, smile
    poor, boor, book, rook, rock, rick, rich
    Now you do the last one.

18. (1) internal medicine (2) heart disease (3) nervous system (4) treatment of syphilis (5) skeletal system and motor organs (6) the skin (7) care of infants and children (8) diseases of females (9) urogenital tract (10) care of women during pregnancy and childbirth.

19. Your dictionary will provide answers even if your memory doesn't. Here's a starter for you: *Titans* were a mighty race of gods who held the heavens against their enemies in what early Greeks thought to be the beginnings of the world. Our word *titantic* means "like a Titan" just as gigantic means "like a giant."

20. (1) Augusta (2) Denver (3) Austin (4) Trenton (5) Nevada (6) Boise (7) Maine (8) Wisconsin (9) Paris (10) Texas (11) Nineveh (12) Idaho

21. (1) systematic way of living (2) customs and manners of a community or group (3) boredom, monotony (4) range, scope, wide variety (5) a harmless pill or liquid (6) finishing point, end of the line (7) for the time being, temporary (8) a composition of words, music, etc. (9) distance from the center of a circle to the edge (10) relative position.

22. (1) g (2) j (3) f (4) a (5) c (6) e (7) i (8) b (9) d (10) h

23. (1) a particle in the blood necessary for clotting
    (2) one who is overly anxious about his or her health

127

(3) related to the vessels that carry fluids such as blood and lymph
(4) to waste away, to wither
(5) destructive, poisonous
(6) emotional shock
(7) stout
(8) directly into a vein (*intravenous* feeding)
(9) a physical ailment caused by emotional stress
(10) unconscious, as if in a coma or stupor

24. (1) origin, development, and behavior of mankind (2) origin, history, and structure of the earth (3) the science of plants (4) the biological science of animals (5) language development (6) study of insects (7) wines (8) human social behavior (9) diseases of the eye (10) disorders of the ear, nose, and throat.

25. Answers are easy, especially if you use your dictionary carefully. For instance, if you were trying to define "antiquary," you would discover that he or she was *not* the keeper of a zoo, or a stamp collector, or a physician treating older people. An "antiquary" is "a student of antiques." Having gone this far, how about looking up *antiques* in your dictionary?

26. (1) a truck (2) candy or dessert (3) hood of a car (4) an elevator (5) a baby carriage (perambulator) (6) apartment (7) a wrench (8) rest room (9) molasses (10) French-fried potatoes (11) a cracker (12) battery (13) paved road (14) trunk of a car (15) fender (16) traffic circle (17) garbage can (18) druggist (pharmacist) (19) suspenders (20) girl

27.

1. Amelia Bloomer
2. A Scottish clan of Argyle
3. The 7th Earl of Cardigan
4. A French play named *Fedora*
5. Jean (from Genoa, where first made)
6. Jules Léotard, French aerialist
7. Charles Macintosh, Scottish chemist
8. Lord Raglan, British soldier
9. denim (serge of French city Nimes)
10. The Earl of Chesterfield

28. Answers are easy if you will use your dictionary. For instance, you can quickly learn that *atlas* comes from the representation of the giant Atlas holding up the heavens, a common feature in sixteenth-century books of maps. Try the other nineteen eponyms in this question. They're easy.

29. (1) e (2) j (3) f (4) i (5) h (6) g (7) a (8) b (9) c (10)d

30.

1. Welsh
2. Arabic
3. Irish
4. Tahitian
5. Choctaw
6. Egyptian
7. Latin
8. Italian
9. Turkish
10. Yiddish
11. French
12. Afrikaans
13. Spanish
14. Haitian
15. Australian
16. Hawaiian
17. German
18. Russian
19. Dutch
20. Persian